# SNICKERING OUT LOUD

Jenny Sauer

Grinding Gears Publishing

Grinding Gears Publishing
www.jennysauer.com

Publisher's Note: This is a work of fiction. Names, characters, places, and incidents are a product of the author's imagination. Locales and public names are sometimes used for atmospheric purposes. Any resemblance to actual people, living or dead, or to businesses, companies, events, institutions, or locales is completely coincidental.

Book Layout ©2013 BookDesignTemplates.com

Snickering Out Loud/ Jenny Sauer. -- 1st ed.
ISBN 978-0-578-13788-9

*Special thanks to my mom and dad. I give them all my thanks and admiration for being the most amazing, supportive parents a kid could ever ask for...*

*Another BIG thanks to the people that contributed to creating the book cover:*

*Photographer-Jeremy Byrd*

*Makeup Artist-Jules Fleming*

*Jewelry-Joyce Hembrough of Duncan & Hoots Jewelers Jacksonville, IL*

# Contents

# ABOUT THE AUTHOR

I like to have fun, but I also like to have alone time. I'm fairly unemotional, matter-of-fact, and brutally honest. I'm an independent thinker and appreciate anyone who is up-front and honest. I look at life logically and look at some aspects of life as different levels of efficiency. The more efficient something is the better the outcome, in my view anyway. I'm really not a fan of dating and look at dating as being efficient, or an inefficient art, in the sense that you get everything out considered controversial in the beginning so as to not waste each other's time. With all of this out of the way, you know at the beginning if it's something that you want to pursue or say, "Next!" In my view, the ideal way to meet people would be if each person came in with their own little pamphlet about family health history, past relationships, their relationships with siblings and parents, etc. You would then be able to read each other's history and views on issues and decide, "Hmmm, I could take a hefty bathroom break with the door open and they would just sigh and walk away."

I wish I found dating more fun, but it's never been something I've really enjoyed because I tell the same stories every time. Every first date is the same, the same questions and the same answers, from myself anyway. I find it monotonous. I have always been a "long-termer" relationship kind of gal. I went from one long relationship to the next, joined Match.com in the middle, and then back to dating people the old-fashioned way. For example, "Frank" is a recurring thread throughout the book. Frank and I were in a relationship for about three and an half years that continued through the cities of Dallas, TX, Little Rock, AR, Oklahoma City, OK, and ended in Los Angeles, CA. You will see, as the reader, his name come up more often due to the fact that I was involved with this dullard in four different cities.

My goal of this book is to have people say, "Oh yeah, that happened to me, I can totally relate." I want people to see these problems and issues then find a way to prevent them from happening, or fixing them before they become out of hand, "nip it in the bud" if you will. I have included a section for women and men on what not to do and what should be done to find that perfect mate. I'm not married, so there will be no marriage advice given. I have been told by many men that I am fairly unemotional, which has to do with being overly logical. I have had girlfriends come and go, girls that are friends, and not in a romantic sense. I have some of the same girlfriends that are the emotional saps type. The emotional saps have provided a very different insight to dating, and provided me with ideas and tips to use myself.

These stories are based upon actual events from friends' experiences and my own. I also hope that most of these can be of use for same-sex couples. I have a lot of gay friends, and some of these problems are not just between a man and a woman but cross over to all relationship types.

As I look back upon my dating life, it makes me smile and laugh, and I hope you do just the same.

This book is about the humorous perils and pitfalls of dating. I have had an interesting, entertaining, and an adventurous life to say the least. I'm writing this to share my stories and to hopefully better educate men and women on the art of dating. Now I'm not pulling a Taylor Swift and writing a story about each and every guy I date and then choose to break up with; this book is purely for entertainment reading, something you can pick up and put down at any time, as well as a guide. It's a fun read at the end of the day because you don't want to be thrown under the bus, let's be honest here, it is what it is (figured I would throw in overused sayings for your amusement).

# CHAPTER ONE

# My Life Story

I grew up on a farm in Riggston, Illinois, and loved every minute of it. I did indeed drive a 4555 John Deere tractor, rake hay, cultivate, mowed a lot, helped feed and raise cattle and pigs. Cattle are more fun than pigs by the way. I helped castrate the cattle and pigs, cleaned out the manure in some cattle areas, showed two steers (castrated bulls) two different years in 4-H during high school, fixed fence, built fence, helped move cattle across the road to other pastures, and the like. This is all thanks to my dad. My dad is like "Super Dad' and still is. He made this girl into a well-rounded individual. My mom helped of course, but the "guy stuff" was all thanks to my dad.

Farming is a great life; I wish everyone could experience what I did. Maybe not so much the castrating animals deal, but the outdoors and freedom is something that a city cannot duplicate in any museum, arboretum, or public park. The way things smell are so different, along with the coloring of the landscape. The stimuli are there, but people that grew up in cities think it's so boring out in the country because they grew up with a completely different type of stimuli. They had constant lights flashing and loud sounds. Out in the rural areas, you learn to hear things better and want to hear things, not cover your ears because the damn train is going by for the second time in one minute. My hearing and sense of smell are ridiculous. Another thing is that stars are absolutely stunning. Every year, on August 9, (I remember this because a girl I have been friends with since we were about four or five years old, we went to gymnastics together and actually lived maybe 0.1 miles from one another) I remember to watch the meteor shower that happens every year on that night. On her birthday one year (Aug. 9), she had a slumber party of about 10-15 girls, and we watched the meteor shower while lying on her trampoline outside. All of us brought a blankie to lie outside and enjoy the light show in the sky. It was a beautiful experience. So every year on her birthday, I remember to watch the meteor shower in whatever city I may be living in at the time.

In the rim of "my" 4555 John Deere. This was considered mine because I enjoyed driving this all the time, but technically, it is my father's tractor.

In the spring and summer, there are the crops, mostly corn and soybeans around my hometown. You get to see the farmers ripping or cultivating, and there is a distinct smell when they're performing this. It's a wonderful dirt smell! It might sound weird but when you smell it, you'll know exactly what I'm talking about. The fresh cut grass smell, which is more prominent & different in the country because the grass is full of different weeds and such on the embankments and ditches, so it's yet another wonderful scent that "stings the nostrils." We, as well as other farmers, cut and bale hay and that has its own beautiful aroma. In the fall, the leaves change, the corn and soybeans take on another color, thereby completely changing the landscape all over again. The harvest season has its own wonderful, distinctive perfume, and then comes winter. One might think it a desolate-looking landscape, but when one takes the time to actually look and pay attention, not just glance, it's beautiful. It's a bleak color palette, but there's something very beautiful in that barren landscape. And when it snows, it's amazing. Around my hometown, the wind picks up pretty good sometimes, and the drifts that the wind creates in the empty fields can be quite spectacular. Fields upon fields of snow, untouched by salt and cars, is mesmerizing. Then we take out the snowmobiles and mess it up some, but that's fun to do after taking in the untouched, snowy landscape.

Us country folk get to watch the corn and soybeans grow, it is amazing to see that process; to my dad and me, we both have said it's like watching your kids grow, only on speed (I added in the speed thing, dad wouldn't say that). The crops that the farmers put in every year are like their children. They take such care in making sure the crops' home, the land, is cultivated the best so it's comfy, cozy, and safe enough for them to grow. The minerals are present in the ground in varying levels so the best fertilizers and chemicals, that may or may not be needed, the farmer would buy because they nurture their crop. This is the farmer's livelihood, not just a fun game. Now I will say that there are some farmers that put the tractor on top speed in order to be the first ones done. I think most tractors can now go up to 18 miles per hour, whoa, watch out! This is stupid because at the end of the year what you obtain and your yields produced is how you and your family are going to survive. This is something that city people might have a harder time grasping initially: Slow down, take pride in what you do and do your best. Don't do something quickly just to get it done, do it with a purpose and you will see that your life will be much less stressed. I do everything with a purpose, now I did just say "everything" granted I have done stupid things, but for the most part, there is a reason behind everything I do. Just because you do something at a slower speed than someone else doesn't mean you aren't being productive, it's called time management people. Much like the saying, "Slow and steady wins the race."

One of my best friends, Samantha, and I in our cattle/pig lot. We made those coveralls "hot." That could mean temperature or physical looks wise.

My relationship with my parents is great. I'm very close to both of them. I call them often and tell them everything. My mom is just like I am, only nicer in the sense that she worked part-time in customer service and will listen to people complain about bringing back a pair of used underwear and not getting a refund for them. I really admire the lack of pride some people possess.

My mom has her limits though. My dad always blamed our incredible arguing skills on the Irish side. Nope, not true. Although my dad is very non-confrontational, you don't want to piss him off. I was also very close to my late grandparents on the Sauer side, and I still very much love my McGrath grandparents. I still love them more than anything to this day. My grandma Sauer didn't put up with any bull. If she didn't like something, you better damn well expect her to tell you what she thought about it, even if you didn't want to hear it. I'm kind of like that; I'm a great mix of both mom and dad. I have an older brother, Danny, and sister, Laura. My brother is seven years older than me, and my sister is four years old than I am. Yes, I am "the baby" but my parents were equal with all three of us. I'm sure their favorite is me of course, just kidding. I remember when my brother would wake me up, and get me out of my crib on Saturday mornings, lay a blankie on the kitchen floor, and we would watch cartoons together. My sister would join us eventually, but she was quite the sleeper and enjoyed sleeping in. I was closest to my brother growing up, then closer to my sister as we got older. It's funny how the family dynamic changes over the years, but there isn't one favored over the other; I'm exceptionally lucky and fortunate to have a family like I do.

Laura, Danny, and me circa 1996. Gotta love the bangs.

# CHAPTER TWO

# What, Do I Look Like A

t?

I have so many people call me almost every day asking for advice or how to handle situations. It's because I tell them the truth and they know that they can count on me to tell them if they look like a dead cow in a dress. "Dr. D bag #2," explained in a later section, told me that men have a hard time opening up and talking about emotions to women. That has never happened to me. I'm not entirely sure why, but they tell me everything. I may think in my mind, "Damn, that was stupid and you shouldn't have done that," but I don't say it while they are pouring their hearts out to me. I know my limits. I tell them what I think of the situation because they honestly want to know why I think the way I do. I don't offer advice unless prompted to do so.

I always joke about making my own bumper sticker "WWJD" with a skinny girl holding a cocktail in one hand and a long cigarette in the other. Just in case, the "J" would be for "Jenny," not "Jesus." I may seem somewhat bitchy, but when it comes to my family and friends, I would die for each and every one of them. When I love, I love hard. If anyone does anything in the slightest to wrong any of my friends, I'm right there taking charge and tell the "bad people" what I have to say. Everyone I have known

7

has said to others, "You don't want to piss Jenny off." It takes a lot to get me to the "pissed off" stage, but mess me with me on purpose, attack a family member or friend, and the gloves come off. No bitch mittens here.

I care a lot for humanity, I really do, but I do not care for stupidity. I hate drama, I have enough friends that have plenty of drama in their lives to make up for what is lacking in mine. A motto I enjoy following: "I don't give a shit." This motto makes my life essentially drama free. If you don't like me, that's great because that more than likely means I don't like you either. You move on, get past it, and grow up. ~~~~ng me more than twice, there is no third strike and you're out, y~~ ~~~~. I only gave one person in my life that option and it's t~~ ~~~~ and best friends. I really can't remember what happened to make ~~ ~~~e touch, I'm sure it was something very insignificant, but she's my "twin." It's funny because my cousin and I look more like sisters than my actual sister and I (or so we have been told).

My cousin, Elizabeth, and I.

My sister, Laura, and I

I want people to see that you can indeed be honest and live a wonderful life. No creating smoke screens and stabbing people in the back, oh come on now! Man up and just say what is on your mind! There are times to tone it down, yes, but for the most part, just be yourself and love your life more than your dog or cat, which I know can be difficult to do at times. I say that because I have a cat, Sylvester, and I love him like he's my furry little son.

My now three-legged cat, Sylvester. He had bone cancer in his right hind leg, so I had it removed. He's doing well, and has always been an exceptional indoor "farm kitty," meaning he was a kitty from our farm.

I enjoy learning, and yes, I actually enjoyed school (nerd alert), but my mom and dad taught my brother, sister, and me to pay attention to everything around you, take it all in, think about it, digest it, and let it marinate and simmer. When you figure out how to do that, you'll see what I'm talking about.

On the topic of my parents, I have the most loving parents in the world. My parents will have been married for 39 years, (this year March 22, 2014) and yes, they do still love each other. My family is very important to me, without them, I could have a high probability of being a very angry person.

My mom and dad, Hunter and Theresa Sauer.

I also grew up Catholic, another aspect of my life that is very important. I was the first girl to be an altar server at my church.

A rosary given to me by Sophie (mentioned later)

I was also always an athlete. I started playing basketball competitively at the local YMCA when I was in third grade and was the only girl on my team. I've always enjoyed playing with the boys, not because I'm attracted to them, but because they are more aggressive and actually play with skill rather than scratching you or pulling your hair because you are prettier than them. I also ran track and played softball in the summers, volleyball for fun, and golf in high school where I was the only girl on the golf team as well. My hometown has a population of 1,800 people, so I never wanted to date anyone from there. The 1,800 place is where I attended grade school and high school (Winchester, Illinois), about eight minutes away from where I grew up. The actual place I grew up in is a small village (Riggston, IL) of seven houses where my great grandfather started a John Deere dealership, which is still a John Deere dealership today, just under different ownership.

I never really hung out in my small town because people always wanted to go to "farm parties." Since there isn't much to do in the small town, the only thing to do was get together and get drunk on someone's farm ground. That was not my idea of fun in high school. I was essentially a good kid. I never did drugs and/or drank to excess. That was until...

When I was 15 years old, almost 16, I went to visit my cousin (pictured before, Elizabeth) for the New Year. I had tasted beer before, but never liked it and never had the desire to drink it. So for the New Year, what did my cousin and I do? We drank to excess. I drank seven Bush, "porkchop in a can," beers in a matter of just a couple hours. I was tanked. That was actually when I had my first kiss, how romantic eh? I passed out on some guys couch and don't remember anything else. All I remember is that my cousin was there to watch over me, thank goodness, and I felt horrible the next day, we both did. My dad was to pick me up from my grandma's house, and when he did, he didn't say one word to me the whole way home. It was about a ten-minute drive home, but it felt like 30. I didn't know my dad knew until we pulled up to our garage and he said, "Did you get thirsty?" Oh man, I thought I was going to die. It was the most horrible feeling I've ever had, my heart sank down to my anus because that's exactly what I felt like, a total ass. I was then grounded for a long time but what I took from that was quite the learning experience: Don't piss off dad. It was the huge disappointment that I caused from my mom and dad that just killed me. After that, I never wanted to drink because the way they looked at me was enough punishment. As I have gotten older, that of course has changed.

I went off to college at the University of Illinois at Urbana-Champaign with hopes to study biology. During my freshman year, I had one other episode of pure drunk excess. For my 19th birthday (you could get into the bars if you were that age there), I went out with a few friends. One of those friends happened to be 25 years old, so he bought all the drinks because the rest of us were 19 years old. I had a blast; however, good things must come to an end and a shitty end this was for my friends. We were walking back home to my dorm and I puked all over some protestant church's steps. A lot of people were walking by and saying "Good job!" "Damn girl!," and so on. So I say in response to the hecklers, "It's ok, I'm Catholic," apparently being drunk AND Catholic are acceptable in my inebriated mind.

Mind you, this street we were walking on was VERY busy. The university cops show up. I don't know how I did it in my drunken stupor, but I pointed out my dorm, gave them my address, and saved my 25 year old friend from getting fined and butt raped in jail. There were two guys and one other girl with me, and the cops asked me if the 25-year-old man bought us our drinks. Somehow I came up with "No, some guys thought we were cute at the bar and bought our drinks." As it ends up, the other two friends, which were underage, had to go to an alcoholic rehab teaching class; I didn't nor did the 25-year-old guy. Oh the irony.

I moved on from biology to a nursing program, and that profession is most certainly not for me. I did clinicals at a hospital, and one time, had to clean up some patient's defecation mess. I asked about how often that happened. I remembered the head nurse telling me that if the CNA (certified nurse assistant) wasn't there on hand, you yourself have to do it. This might sound as though this profession is beneath me. NO, far from it. In my view, if I take four years of college and spend a lot of money on a bachelor's degree, I don't believe I should have to do that sort of work. Do I appreciate the CNA's and what they do? Of course, but four years and thousands of dollars should guarantee that I would not be cleaning the excrement from someone's rear. I appreciate nurses a whole hell of a lot more because they put up with a lot of shit, pun intended. Just like, "There is someone for everyone," there is also a job for everyone.

I decided to go back to my initial major of biology because I loved it and missed it. I always wanted to be podiatrist, so I started shadowing a couple different doctors. One doctor was a gynecologist, and what was really weird was that I loved it. I think the woman's "lady parts" are gross, but it never bothered me seeing other women and their naughty bits. It was something that was fascinating to me and it was a learning experience. And what's really funny is that I shadowed a podiatrist after shadowing the gynecologist, and right after that I was completely grossed out by the old people that had diabetes. The podiatrist was cleaning the patients' toenails, and to me that was the most disgusting thing; but seeing a woman that had a yeast infection wasn't nearly as gross. Now it was still gross, but I could stomach that over cleaning out an old person's toenails that hadn't been cleaned out for six months plus. It makes me want to puke in my mouth right now writing about it.

What this experience taught me was that I wasn't always right. I might've had an idea that was what I wanted, but I obviously just proved myself wrong. I hate being wrong, but when I prove myself wrong, it's quite the experience and I love it for some reason, I guess you could call it a love-hate relationship with myself. I learned so much that one year and it taught me to follow my heart and gut. I really think they are both intertwined, but I went with what I felt, it was pretty damn amazing. This was a time where I look back and smile because I did what I wanted and followed my heart, something my parents have always supported. They made their grumblings known, but they never discouraged me. By them doing this, I learned much faster because I was learning by my own mistakes; not by someone else telling me. So I went for it, and after graduating college, I followed my ex's (Frank's) twin sister to Dallas (Sophie), and oh boy, that was an experience…

# Oh the Cities in Which I Have Tripped Gracefully

# CHAPTER THREE

# Dallas

So here comes Dallas. Frank's twin sister, Sophie, got a job in Dallas and asked me to move with her. Their parents (Sophie and Frank's) wanted me to go and live with her to make sure that she would be okay, someone to watch out for her so to speak. I can say that the parents weren't exactly confident in their daughter's ability to take care of herself, let alone protect herself. I met Sophie after I met Frank in college. Sophie was bubbly, loud and talked ALL the time. You'd think she would make a lot of friends by being such a social butterfly. Here was the problem with her and I cohabitating: I'm not bubbly and loud, and I enjoy napping. You don't know something until you try it though right? Anyway, this isn't a "Let's bash Sophie" moment, she really was nice and fun to be around, but our personalities didn't mesh well for cohabitation. We had some very fun times together, and I don't regret any of those experiences with her.

I enjoyed being independent and making friends on my own, and I mean that in the sense of having my own friends and not constantly being around her. I like having my own escape; it doesn't mean I didn't like her, but what I mean is that I enjoy having my "own thing" without having to drag someone along every time I do something. I take pride in creating my own path and doing things in which I make my own mistakes and learn from them. While I was in Dallas, I worked at a couple fitness clubs, private Pilates training and performed all the other nineteen certifications I had in the fitness realm.

Dallas was a good time and I met some good people, but I can say that Dallas was pretty superficial. Someone once told me that it's the home of the $30,000 millionaire; I can see that. I can also say that the amount of plastic faces were about the same as in Los Angeles. The hair and makeup, damn, it was like I was being a spectator in a beauty pageant 24/7, it was pretty ridiculous. I didn't want to hurt Sophie's feelings, which is precisely why I'm telling you to never live with a best friend or a sibling's sibling, but I needed to move out; I liked her, but I liked her more when I didn't live with her. I enjoy visiting Dallas now, and the shopping is pretty fantastic there. My best friend, Gina, lives there now and we have had some good times in The Big D.

While I was living in Dallas, Frank was in Little Rock, Arkansas working on graduate studies because he didn't get into medical school his first try (can't say I'm too surprised). I wanted to be closer to him since we had just started dating at the end of our senior school year in college, and we hadn't been together much. He allowed his parents to tell him what to do, or at least sway him in a way to do what they wanted, mostly what dad wanted. Frank was a dreamer and had a creative mind; he wanted to do so many different things but couldn't decide on one, so his dad decided for him. I'm sure they would tell this story very differently, but I know what I saw and heard; he was definitely not living his dream according to himself.

# CHAPTER 4

# Oh Little Rock'iness

I got a job doing clinical research at a lab in Little Rock, and moved to Little Rock to be with Frank.

Me in the lab with some dry ice…and blonde highlights.

Oh Little Rock, the people I met there are still life-long friends. If it were in another location, I might have just stayed there; however, there was a shooting one day, in the middle of the afternoon, in the parking lot of the labs where I worked. That didn't exactly make me feel comfortable and safe. The downtown area was nice, but once you experienced it, that was that. Once again, Frank complained about not having any friends. Now there is a pattern here: he isn't good at making friends. He was only good at keeping his high school friends, now that says something- to me anyway. I had to deal with that in addition to him getting jealous that I would be invited out to do things because he would have to stay behind and study.

One very "eye-opening" moment was when I found out I was to be published in a couple scientific journals. Oddly enough, he wasn't really all that happy for me. The conversation eventually turned into, "I'm working so hard on my research and I can't get anything to work, and I can't get published."-Frank. It was a really nice "fuck you" from him, so I celebrated by talking to people that were actually happy for me. It seemed as though every problem I had, Frank was able to manipulate it to the point of, "Well in MY situation..." As to why I continued to stay in this relationship is still quite the mystery to me, all I can conclude is that I was stupid and ignorant. I was asked from people there in Little Rock, my Alma Mater, Oklahoma City, and many times after we broke up, by others, "Why, why, why were you dating Frank?" Well you know, I don't know. I disappointed myself, thereby teaching myself quite the lesson and what "not look for in a man."

The lab in Little Rock I worked in was great; except for this guy I called "PruSHITum." That is mostly his name, but all you need to know is that he was a total dickhead. I was one of the few white people in the lab, and I was completely cool with that. I got along very well with the boss. She was a very smart and exceptionally nice woman who was running the lab. I was VERY proud to have a female boss. She was very nice to me, and I respected her greatly. I was also great friends with a graduate student and another man in there; the three of us had some good times making fun of people. PruSHITum, I found out after I decided to leave, would time my lunches and tell on me when I was a few minutes late after the 45-minute allotted lunchtime. Funny enough because my boss never told me about it because she knew I lived right next door in the dorms. I walked home for lunch every day, she knew that, she didn't care. PruSHITum's wife worked in the lab and she definitely wore the pants in their relationship. There was another girl, around my age, and me in the lab, and we were directly under P. Shit. That was his only time that he could go on a power trip and get away with being an asshole because I know his wife would've reamed him a new one if he stepped on her toes. The other girl was much more submissive, so P.Shit went after her more because I was obviously a lot more work to control. Thankfully it got to a point where I just couldn't take it anymore from him and decided that I would leave soon.

Frank was then accepted into med school in Oklahoma City, and what makes me snicker some, is that he obtained a very small, and I mean very small, percentage minority card and conveniently was admitted into medical school after his parents obtained the minority card for him. I had put in so much time and money into this guy that I continued following him wherever he went. After I look back on it all, I loved him, but didn't really love him; know what I mean? You can love someone but it's very different actually being "in love" with someone. I decided that I was going to move to Oklahoma City at some point, but in the meantime, had a good time hanging out with my awesome nerdy research friends. The other research people I hung out with were all researching graduate students, around my age and slightly older, but they sure knew how to have a good time. They all still do research today and made fun of Frank so much; it was quite entertaining. One of my best research buds, a very crude but downright hilarious Turk, would laugh and laugh about how he couldn't believe I was with Frank. I actually visited the Turk and his wife a couple years ago, and he's still the same, and I couldn't believe he found a woman to put up with his bullshit, but she's perfect for him and lets him be him. I hung out with that research crowd a lot, and even played on a kickball team where we named ourselves the "Acid Base Runners"(very fitting nerd name); we were good. That compliment may or may not be very biased.

Part of the kickball team in Little Rock, AR.

We would drink every game; it was a ton of fun. A bunch of adults playing kickball is funny anyway, but adding alcohol into the mix was even more funny and entertaining. I decided to move back home to the farm for a little bit in order to find a job in Oklahoma City.

# CHAPTER 5

# Okie Oklahoma

A picture I took of an ice storm while I was living in Oklahoma City.

I moved to Oklahoma City, against my better judgment, and started working at a health club there. I taught fitness classes and did personal training. I had my own apartment; it was okay but I basically lived with Frank most of the time anyway. The health club was close to his medical school, so it worked out just fine. I had a good time at the gym, my boss sucked, but the people I worked with were very enjoyable. I met a lot of people while working at the gym; it was a fun time, but not rewarding. I wasn't really using my brain, so I got bored and felt like I was becoming more stupid by the passing hours. There was a guy there, "Oil dude," a patron, and he came to my classes a lot

25

because he liked me. I knew exactly what he was doing, but I am never one to cheat, so I kept it at "just friends," even though I knew he wanted something else. He was a nice guy with a "loud as hell" voice.

The trend of being with Frank continued. People in Oklahoma City asked why in the hell I was with Frank. I started getting the hint loud and clear at this point, but already knew the end was coming so I just didn't put any more work into it. Frank had such good friends (sarcasm) that a lot of them tried to date me, even contacted me after Frank and I broke up. This phenomenon happened in every city. There were a couple guys that were quite persistent during and after Frank. It was in Oklahoma City when I decided to go out to Los Angeles and pursue a dream I've always had…acting.

# CHAPTER 6

# Los Angeles

This is the view of the Hollywood sign from behind looking down upon the Hollywood Hills. I would hike the trail that lead to the Hollywood sign often.

I moved out to Los Angeles, stayed with a woman, Tina, who was actually from St. Charles, Illinois, and she was great. She had two dogs, she was maybe 10-15 years older than me, had a nice house with a pool, and overall she had a great disposition. It was a shame when after three months of living with her she got a job in New York and needed to move, which meant I needed to move as well. Unlike most people I met in Los Angeles, she was solid, probably because she was from the Midwest, but she searched and found an apartment for me. That was one of the nicest things anyone has ever done for me anywhere. I didn't have to do a thing; she found the apartment and got it all set up. I only had to meet the landlord and sign the papers. I really do hope she is doing well, and her two boys (dogs); she's someone that has a very good heart and still very special to me

So I was able to enjoy her pool for a while, but then moved into my own studio. After about six or seven months, I decided I should probably buy a bed rather than sleep on my air mattress. I really didn't care, I was okay with it because it really was comfortable and why spend money on a bed when I wasn't sure how long I was going to be in that space? I made do just fine and was happy in my little space.

I had no background in theatre and acting whatsoever. The high school plays always seemed odd to me. Overall, I did not want to spend extra time out of school to spend with the people in the plays -just not my "thang." It's kind of like being in band, I tried it in grade school and it still wasn't cool to me. I used my dad's old coronet that he used back in his day, probably for one year like me, and said, "This is not for me." I enjoy listening to people that are good instrumentalists, but I myself simply do not have the drive to become a good instrumentalist.

I was a stage manager for a play in college. I remember the try-outs, weird that this would be a precursor to me going into acting, but it was for the lead character (go big or go home right?) because I was not about to half-ass this. The lead character was supposed to speak with a southern accent. I still remember after the audition, the people in the auditorium congratulated me and said that I had a great accent and did so well. I thought I had it in the bag, but, like I find out how casting works, the teacher went with a girl that she had worked with before. I understand it now, but that main girl stunk, and I'm not saying this out of being bitter, but rather my family and friends came to this play and were not impressed with the lead talent. It was a good experience because I got to see how it worked and some of the jargon used. That is what I could remember of it five years later whenever I joined the acting circuit.

Los Angeles was a big step, and I didn't realize that until after I moved back to Chicago. I always thought a lot of people moved to Los Angeles to pursue a dream; apparently they decide to do that when they have more experience behind them. I use the creative side but don't let it override my logical, business-savvy side. Of course, I did my research before I left. I take risks, but calculated ones. I learned that you are your own business and to not expect your agent to get all the work for you. I also learned of the amount of transplants in and out of Los Angeles every day, not just every month, but every day there is a ridiculous amount of people moving in and out of that place. It is also a place where people believe "the grass is always greener," meaning they can always find someone else that is, in their eyes, better.

Whether or not that is true, it is the home of the 40-year-old single man. I have never met so many older single men in one city. They say that the girls always look the same because they continually think they can get 18-to-20-year-old girls, and that these girls will actually stick with them. HA! Oooooh, that always makes me laugh. Those young girls would cheat on them nonstop. Los Angeles is a place full of beautiful people, and that means beautiful men as well. You think a hot 21-year-old girl is going to stick with old balls over there and be faithful? You have got be kidding me if you think that's true. The young ladies know how to have a good time too, and do they ever know how to have a good time, a little too much sometimes.

One of the crazy nights out in Hollywood; this was taken at Beacher's Madhouse, located at the Roosevelt Hotel. Now that is a crazy and fun place to go.

Los Angeles, most especially Hollywood, is a place of excess and not reality. I had friends I would call my "three month friends." It's much like dating in that you know after a period of three months what type of person you're dating. Some crazy starts to seep out and you start picking up on things because you're getting over that high of being infatuated. Well, that same phenomenon happened with friends. I was lucky and smart in the sense that I made the right friends. I made friends with some club promoters and was genuinely thankful and appreciative of what they did for me; that meaning getting me into some of the hottest clubs and free drinks. I thanked everyone that did something for me and I meant it. That's the key here Los Angeles people, I come in with none, zero, zilch experience and am actually pretty successful in a short period of time, and it's all because I meant what I said. I didn't blow smoke up anyone's arse. I didn't need to suck a guy's man parts to get anywhere; I used my brain with a decent helping of my looks. This time in L.A. was really the first time I had to use my looks, and it was terribly uncomfortable. My parents put a lot of emphasis on the subject of education, so I never actually thought to use my looks to get anywhere because looks do indeed fade.

I will give you one example of the type of person I met while in L.A. I was on the set for "The Mentalist," and this girl with a very annoying voice, talked and talked the entire time. I just so happened to be listening to her mindless babble when she said, and this is true folks, "I was driving to set this morning and I saw this truck. The truck was watering the palm trees in the middle thingy in the road! I had no idea they watered the trees here!" My initial reaction was to throw a piece of cheese at her, but I really wanted to eat that piece of cheese, so I said, very loudly so the whole crowd of people could hear me, "You do know we are basically living in a desert right?" She says, "Well yeah." I say, "Didn't you also say that you grew up in Pasadena?" She says, "Yes." I then continue to remain silent. I'm sure I made a "you are incredibly out-of-touch/stupid face," but it doesn't matter. The main point is that I met a lot of people exactly like that girl. To combat that, I did meet people that knew the city of angels went around watering the trees.

One of my first jobs, while not being in the union of SAG (Screen Actor's Guild), was a commercial for Justin Timberlake's 901 tequila. I will tell you, reader, he is one of the most amazing people I have met, celebrity-wise, while out in Hollywood. He's exceptionally good-looking as well. I was chosen out of the cattle call (a big group of extras at a set) to be taken upstairs and possibly be chosen as a principle in the commercial. I thought that was pretty cool because I didn't have to sit in the horrible metal chairs anymore. Anyway, I get up there and start talking to people involved in the commercial and people close to JT. I was also getting my hair and makeup fixed as well; now that was a pretty nice perk. The people in the room were cool, great actually. As I was sitting there, Justin came up to me and introduced himself. I remember thinking to myself, "Ummmm, duh, I know who you are." I of course never said that out loud, but thought that it showed just how humble Justin was. I sat and talked to his friends for a long time. I had a great time until they found out I wasn't union and would have to pay extra (Taft-Hartley me) then I was thrown in "featured extra" parts. The Taft-Hartley just means that production would have to pay a certain amount of money and you would automatically be accepted into the union. It's a substantial amount of money, and probably enough at the time that I wasn't worth spending that amount upon. Meh, it was all good. I had finally met a celebrity that wasn't an asshole; he knew who he still was and where he came from. He had to start somewhere too, and he worked his ass off to get to where he is today. I also worked with him again on the movie "In Time." He was just as nice on that movie set as he was on the set of his tequila commercial. He's totally my type, it's a shame he's married.

There was one club promoter, I think he was a Mexican mix, and he was terribly attractive. We made out in his BMW one night; he was pretty good at the making out part. He helped me and introduced me to his friends. I felt anyway, even if he didn't, that he cared some and wanted to make sure I had a good time. I also had this Bolivian girlfriend that was loud and annoying. One night, she made a big scene about not wanting to go to The Supper Club in Hollywood because she wanted to go somewhere else. I remember thinking to myself, "You have GOT to be kidding me right now. We are five girls deep, all good looking, and we have this handsome promoter that is getting us in because he's being nice to me; we won't have to worry about paying for anything, umm, what's wrong with this picture you stupid bish?" My promoter friend told her what's up, and frankly I was impressed he did. I'm not entirely sure if that's the night we made out in his car, but regardless, we went to that club and had a great time. I thanked him for everything, and he knew I meant exactly what I said. He also knew I wasn't trying to get with him in order to get any perks. I sincerely thought of him as a friend, an attractive one to say the least, but a friend nonetheless. So my Bolivian friend went in, got some free drinks in her and started bitching about wanting to go somewhere else. This was a trend with her because she wanted to do whatever she wanted and didn't care about anyone else. She needed to be in control, well that doesn't work out so well when you're friends with someone that has a mind of their own as well. I think she ended up leaving; I don't remember and don't care. I'm still in touch with that promoter on Facebook, and a lot of people from Los Angeles to this day.

Los Angeles was a great experience, it's not ALL bad. I simply couldn't take the superficial, backstabbing stuff. I enjoy honesty and bluntness, both of which do not exist in Los Angeles proper. Some areas outside of Los Angeles, such as Hermosa Beach, Redondo Beach, and Manhattan Beach, are great. I would escape to that area on the weekends to not think of the city stuff. My mom came out to visit one time and we had one of the best vacations I've ever had.

My mom with the Golden Gate Bridge in the background while standing at Alcatraz.

One day, my mom and I decided to take a drive to San Francisco and on the way back, drive on the PCH (Pacific Coast Highway/Highway 1). We had such a great time. We didn't have anything really planned, but enough planned where we wouldn't be stranded without a place to stay. On our way, we stopped at this place in Santa Cruz called "The Mystery Spot." The people that work there claim a small area defies the laws of physics and gravity. One of the illusions, pictured, is where people seemingly are standing level yet look as though they are standing in slanted positions. There were other examples of illusions, but it was a fun "spot" to visit for sure.

Mom and I at "The Mystery Spot" in Santa Cruz, CA. We were on an even plane, but doesn't look like it right?

Yep, that's me in a bathroom inside Alcatraz.

One of our original plans was to see the town of San Francisco and Alcatraz. Before seeing Alcatraz, we of course had a little cocktail before the trip because we had to wait a while until the next boat arrived. We "yucked" it up on the tour and laughed the whole time.

We were then supposed to stay at Big Sur, which was highly recommended by Tina, the woman I first lived with in CA. My mom and I had a little cabin reserved and upon our arrival, my mom and I thought, "Damn, maybe we should've brought a gun because there are definitely bears out here in the middle of nowhere." Of course we didn't, but it was kind of creepy for sure. The cabin was nice, but the appeal of this place was that there were no TVs or Internet in the rooms.

Part of our cabin at Big Sur.

Here's the thing, I'm sorry, kind of but not completely, but mom and I couldn't take it. We can amuse ourselves, but there are modern technologies that people enjoy for a reason. I suppose this place would be good for couples. I just so happen to enjoy sitting on a couch, curled up with my man watching TV. You can sit out on the porch and enjoy the night sky, but when you're worried about what types of feral creatures are lurking in the woods, it's definitely not quite that relaxing. The silence really was killing us. Eventually, we went out on our computers and were able to entertain ourselves in the main cabin area that had an Internet connection.

The next day, we continued on down Highway 1. It was absolutely beautiful. I recommend this trip to ANYONE. The Highway 1 is absolutely stunning. It can be scary at times, yes, but absolutely breathtaking. There was a waterfall that Tina had told me about on that route. The waterfall actually wasn't too far from Big Sur traveling south.

The beautiful waterfall off the 1 highway.

It was gorgeous by that waterfall. It sounded beautiful and we even saw dolphins! Yes, this was like a romance novel coming to life, only I was with my mom. That makes me laugh, but really, she is the perfect traveling companion and she really is one of my best friends now. She was a parent when she was supposed to be, and now people think we sound exactly alike, which we kind of do I suppose, but she's a lot of fun to hang out with because I'm basically hanging out with myself. I can't go wrong there and I'm definitely biased, she's cool and a lot of my friends seem to think so too.

After leaving Big Sur, we drove through Carmel, I would totally buy a house there, Monterrey, and all of those pretty coastal towns. We then decided to stop at the Hearst mansion. This is a MUST-SEE people; it was awesome. The main pool in the mansion is a work of art in itself. Stop and take the tour, it's gorgeous and the architecture is pretty spectacular as well. We then rolled back into Los Angeles to my apartment. While back in my apartment enjoying TV, there was actually quite the scare being reported on a local Los Angeles news stations that part of the Highway 1 fell into the ocean. Good thing we missed that eh?

It was probably after that trip I decided to go online to IKEA and pick out a bed. I ordered the bed and mattress online and assembled the entire thing myself. I was so damn proud of myself I think I drank a bottle of wine with my party of "me, myself, and I," then watched TV afterward. Now that is my idea of a perfect celebration. I love celebrating in the comfort of my own home in sweatpants; nothing beats a pair of good sweatpants.

I figured out how to navigate the acting world by working, doing research, and submitting myself for jobs. Ninety-five percent of the work I obtained in Los Angeles was because of my due diligence, not because I had someone else doing it for me. It's called a job for a reason; you have to work at it. I don't have any family members or friends that are in the industry to get me anywhere. I enjoy taking the harder path, sometimes, because it forces you to learn. If someone does something for you all the time, what happens when they aren't there anymore? Well I'll tell you what happens; you're up the massive whitewater river without a paddle and life vest. I did mostly extra work and I loved it. Some actors say it's beneath them to do extra work. Really? I'm pretty sure you had to start somewhere; no matter how privileged you may have been when starting in the biz.

Now joining the union, the Screen Actors Guild (SAG) at the time I joined, is really the best thing ever. Once you're a union background performer, you are treated much, much better, and the pay increase is quite nice. I was a "must-join" into the union because I had booked "The Hangover, Part II" and needed to be in SAG, otherwise the producer and casting agent would have been fined. When it came to being on "The Hangover, Part II", I of course wanted to work on the movie, so that meant paying into the union so I wasn't blacklisted and the casting guy not be fined as well. I always wanted to meet Bradley Cooper in person, and he is indeed just as attractive in person as he is in photos. I had been in "Project X," "Water for Elephants," and various TV shows like "CSI Miami" and "The Mentalist." I actually had to audition for most of the extra parts I was cast in. I was lucky enough to be a "featured extra," so I was getting booked on union projects left and right.

On most of the sets, I made friends with the crew people; here is my reasoning: 90% of actors are odd, eclectic, narcissistic, or not living in reality. Having said that, there are some good, down-to-earth actors, they just happen to be a rarer find. There's something about Los Angeles that gets people into their own heads too much and they lose sight of the bigger picture. It isn't their world and everyone else is just living in it, but after being there for a while, they tend to think so. Now the crewmen/crewwomen, on most sets, were "normal." They seemed to have a more blue-collar type of attitude I suppose, and not really concerned about being seen and noticed. They were there because they genuinely loved their job. I really appreciated what they did because there is no way I would be making a small wage for being a boom person and holding a fuzzy microphone over my head for 14 hours. You really have to love those fuzzy mics if you enjoy holding them over your head for long periods of time, days in a row. I'm sure the "boom guys/gals" have excellent looking shoulder muscles. It is from these crew members where I learned most everything. Like I've mentioned before, I'm very self-aware and pay attention to everything, so I learned the jargon and who the "DP" (director of photography) and "PA" (production assistant) are, what "marks" to hit and when to hit them. For example, when the crew yells, "Speed!" the camera turns on to start recording, this is NOT when you (as an actor) first begin moving. It is indeed only whenever the director yells "Action!" Now that makes sense, but to a lot of background people that don't pay attention, they never seemed to grasp and fully understand that concept.

My best friend, Gina, and I on Two Rodeo Drive.

I worked enough on sets that I could sustain a decent living out there; it was fun and total ride of a lifetime. I worked on the Warner Brothers lot, that was with "Project X" and that was a fun time. It was a lot of night shoots, but the flamethrower stuntman was pretty cool. Also, watching a brand new Mercedes being driven into the pool was very entertaining as well. I actually worked on all of the major studio lots, and I didn't pay for the tours, I was actually paid to be there. Seeing the lots and recognizing countless movies I had grown up watching was simply awesome. I would NEVER trade that experience for anything. I very simply could not take the lifestyle of Los Angeles and constantly being surrounded by it. I needed a break. People would dress up to go to the grocery store; screw that, I wore my workout clothes. I was ready to move back home and check out the Chicago market.

# CHAPTER 7

# Naperville & Chicago, IL

It had been about seven years, give or take a few months, where I was able to drive home whenever I wanted to in order to see my family. My sister had given birth to twins, Andy and Emmy, and I wanted them to know me. They are the first grandchildren in my family, and the cutest, smartest damn little kids.

I decided to move to Naperville, based upon family members that grew up around the area, because I wanted a nice mix, a compromise if you will, because I had lived in so many cities and I was tired. I love free parking, and I will always love free parking. I think it is absolutely absurd to pay to park. You paid enough for that car, you pay for the gas in your car, you pay the insurance, and pay taxes to support public places and street needs, so why in the hell should you pay for parking?! That's my own "schtick." Plus, I enjoy a sense of calm. The sounds of the city and constant moving are not calming to me. I do like quiet, it doesn't have to be "hearing a pin drop quiet," but just enough so my mind can be at ease and not feel anxious all the time hearing so many sounds. I don't need a lot of stimuli to be entertained; a TV showing some trash reality shows and movies are enough for me. I have friends that love the sounds of the city, and good for them. I enjoy going into the city and visiting them because I get to come back to my free parking space and sleep peacefully. Naperville is such a beautiful city, and the downtown area is actually an area that people use. It isn't there just to have a "downtown" but rather a destination and a place to go. It's clean, safe, and family friendly. Apparently, it makes me an old person because I like the suburbs. Now this is why I enjoy the burbs: If it's family-friendly, you can expect it to be cleaner and safer right? Yeah, I don't hear of people feeling safe living around crack houses, but the park next door looks nice...ish. I don't mind driving either; since I grew up out in the middle of nowhere, I HAD to drive everywhere, so it's not a big deal to me. It takes me 30 to 45 minutes to get into the city, depending upon traffic. I don't mind because again, I know I'm coming back to my nice comfy place with free parking. If there isn't much going on, or I'm not being booked on anything, I simply take a three hour drive south to home. If I happen to get called for a casting or audition while home on the farm, then I can very easily drive back to Chicago. This is one time in my life where I truly am happy. I've been so fortunate to be able to do what I feel is right, follow a dream, and actually see the success from working at it and not giving up. This is the hardest and best job there is out there. It's always a challenge, (challenging to me anyway) because I'm always learning and you never know what will happen. I've never been a patient person, so this career path has definitely made me more aware of what it means to be patient.

I'm still not 100% there with being patient, but at least I'm a work in progress when it comes to learning how to be.

Me in front of "Cloud Gate"; referred to as "The Bean" by every Chicagoan in Millennium Park.

Chicago is a different market than Los Angeles and New York. It's a much smaller niche thereby making it harder to meet people in the biz. In Los Angeles, 90% of the people living there had something to do with the entertainment industry, so it was much easier to make connections. The opportunities in Chicago are much greater because you don't have 500 people going after one role. The parts you are offered to audition for are much bigger, hence me booking my first national commercial for the "Swiffer Steamboost" in Chicago. How crazy is that?! Three and an half years of being in the entertainment business, with absolutely zero background in acting, and I booked a national commercial.

Granted not all of my acting friends were truly happy about me booking that, but for the most part, most of them were because they all knew that I worked at it and didn't talk myself up to people. I'm honest and I tell people how it is, I don't pretend to be something I'm not. Chicago still has the Midwestern mentality and I meet so many nice people on sets and in classes. The city itself is gorgeous, and the food here is hands down the best in the country. I can't say the same for Los Angeles food. I am not about to take shots of wheatgrass because some famous celebrity did it for three weeks, and they claim that's what made them lose 15 pounds. Well no kidding you lost 15 pounds because you turned yourself into a damn rabbit for three weeks. The whole cleansing thing is another issue; I'm not a huge fan of it because I believe that is how some people obtain new allergies to food because, yes, you are getting rid of "toxins" and bad stuff that may be sitting there being comfortable on their "toxic couch" in your intestines, BUT you're also getting rid of the good stuff too. If you're feeling bloated for a couple days, just take a laxative, but don't continually flush out all the good stuff because you want to lose weight. That water weight is going to come back you know.

Chicago is still a pleasant, clean city with nice people. People here will hold the door for you, say "Thank you" when you do something that is common courtesy, and smile and say "Hi" on the street while walking downtown. It's a crazy thing for such a large city, but there are still some good people out there.

I've come a long way and have accomplished a lot in my short lifespan, I'll be turning the big 3-0 in a couple weeks, and I'm happy about it. I'm proud to not look my age, for one thing, but for another, I haven't wasted my life living it according to others. I have the most wonderful parents a kid could ask for who have supported me through each and every decision I've made. Of course they weren't happy about every single one, but they knew and had enough confidence in me that I would figure it out and fix it on my own. That is the one thing I will forever be grateful for from them; they let me be me and had trust in me to figure it out without them doing everything for me. It was the same for dating, they didn't like every guy, but they let me test it out, gave me advice when I asked, and I learned from each and every one. My whole family and I look back and laugh at my dating career, in a good way because there was never a reason to take things so personally that it would affect my psyche, just move on and learn from it. We have plenty of material to make fun of, and I hope that my stories will thoroughly entertain you. Cheers!

My sister, Laura, and I while in Vegas with our half-yard delightful sippers. *clink

# My Relationship History and "Serial Dating" Stage

# CHAPTER 8

# Ray Ray

I started dating a friend of mine when I was a senior in high school funnily named Ray Ray. We were each other's first sexual partner. To me, that was the best thing because neither person had more experience than the other. We both learned together and didn't feel like the other person knew more than the other. When you're under 20 years old, I believe that is the way virginity should be taken. If you're 25 and haven't gotten laid, then either you are a great Christian or are lacking in the dating skills department. You ever see "The 40 year old Virgin?" 'nough said. I went to school at the University of Illinois in Champaign-Urbana and had two horrible roommate experiences during my first year. I've learned a lot about women over my short life span, but this first year of school taught me a lot. I lived in Newman Hall, the all Catholic dorm where students had the highest GPA on campus. It was a perfect breeding ground for dorks, and I was one of them. The first roommate I had was a senior civil engineering student. Yes, I spelled all of that correctly, she was a senior college student still living in the dorms. She had a leather Star Wars jacket and maybe one friend in the dorm. My best friend and cousin (Elizabeth) called one day and thought a man answered the phone, but nope, it was my roommate. She was a nice girl, but never left the room, even when my boyfriend Ray Ray came to visit. I couldn't hack that situation anymore and found this girl I thought I could get along with in my English classes. That was a big mistake. She was an ex-cheerleader from an all-girls Catholic school from the Chicagoland area. To me, I needn't say more, however, I will tell you. She left her underwear all over the floor, wore sweatpants and no makeup to classes, and had a boyfriend at another school that her parents didn't know they saw each other many nights. I had my Ray Ray staying one weekend and that just so happened to be the same weekend my roommate's parents came. The mom got mad at me because she thought that was so horrible I had my boyfriend staying overnight in our shared dorm room. Well, little did they know that their sweet innocent child was quite the party girl and stayed overnight with her boyfriend quite often. She also had many, and what I mean by "many" is A LOT, of empty hard liquor bottles displayed on the top of her desk. Nothing yells "classy" more than a multitude of empty hard liquor bottles displayed for your guests. I also had received a phone call from her boyfriend late one night to go and pick her up over at a frat house because she was claiming that she almost got raped. Well, in my opinion, if you get wasted drunk and ride on a massive bus full of young drunk frat guys, you are asking for trouble. I still went over and picked her up, but feeling sorry for her was not happening at that time, and never did. She was a very disrespectful roommate, and I had lingering resentment from how her mom treated me. The room was mine as well; I had the right to have whomever over. I wasn't disrespectful in the sense of taking up her space or spending all the time in the room. Also, any man or woman that wakes up five minutes before being somewhere, and doesn't put on regular pants? I have zero respect for those people. If you're going for a workout and have pants over workout pants because it's cold, or whatever, that's fine because you more than likely took five to ten minutes to look decent. You don't have to look gorgeous by any means, but for crying out loud, put on something other than a pair of sweatpants that clearly look as though you slept in them. Needless to say, she was never a roommate of mine again.

Ray Ray is still a best friend of mine. We talk and text on occasion. He is the ONLY guy I would ever stay friends with while being in a relationship with someone else. It's because we were friends before we started dating. I still love him and always will.

# CHAPTER 9

# Hank

Moving on from that school, I started dating someone else that I actually ended up getting engaged to, Hank. He was a "good ol' boy" from my small town area. He was an electrician that didn't believe in college and wanted to get married at age 23. I was 21 and thought "Eh, what the hell, he's a nice guy, my parents like him, why not?" I also got to design my engagement ring at our jeweler, so that was a plus. The jeweler ended up calling me and letting me know it was ready. So that blew the whole surprise of getting proposed to. So what happened you might ask? He proposed to me in the kitchen at my farmhouse I was living in at the time. Pretty romantic I must say. I planned a wedding, and called it off twice. Yeah, I felt pretty bad for the guy because that isn't a very nice thing to do, but I knew it wasn't right. The last straw in deciding whether or not to stay with him came whenever I told him about how much I wanted to travel. Hank said, and I quote, "Why would you need to travel when you can just read and see it in a book?" I was done. I couldn't take "narrow-minded man" anymore. He lived with me in my farmhouse for about one and a half years, the span of time we were together. He then decided to move out, but not away…

You know when you break up with someone they normally go away? Yeah, this guy didn't. Hank basically thinks of my now 64-year-old dad as one of his best buddies. I will say my dad is a pretty cool guy, but for crying out loud, find friends your own age. Hank wasn't very social, and when he drank, I truly was embarrassed to be his girlfriend. It was a few summers ago, but he had since moved into one of our rental houses and continued to help my dad out on the farm. This was is perfectly fine, but keep your clutter at your own place. Hank started storing his stuff at my dad's shop and basically treated our family property as his to use freely. There are many little things that he did, such as four-wheeling with friends drunk upon our property without my dad's permission or knowledge. I think these things started to end as Hank got older and realized how idiotic it was, but I can't say that with 100% certainty. My dad is extremely non-confrontational and just a nice guy, too nice sometimes. One thing I will add is that my dad isn't stupid nor a pushover. He knows exactly what is going on but would much rather avoid conflict and let it go, something I have yet to master. So my dad wasn't going to "get him into trouble" so to speak.

One summer when I was home, I thought I should say something on my dad's behalf. My dad also would have been completely okay with me not speaking for him; he actually would've told me to not say anything and to just let it go. Hank had a shoddy, trashy trailer, one of those you hook on the back of truck, and he stored it down in our shop parking area outside. Now where Hank lives, it has a large yard, and a large enough area to park his junk. Well he said that he was keeping it there for a couple weeks because all of the tools needed to work on it were there at our shop. My late grandfather, with whom I was extremely close to, told him one day to move it. Well Hank didn't. So one fine summer day I'm down there and see this girl (she had to have been maybe four to five years younger than me) washing off the trailer. I was with a farm hand at the time, and I said, "Who the fuck is that?" I said it in that way because anyone at our shop is someone that is supposed to be there and someone that I would know. Granted there have been a couple times I wasn't sure who the person might be, but that's twice during my lifetime. That means I normally know everyone that is at our "shop."

Come to find out, the girl was a girlfriend of Hank's younger brother. I went up to her and asked her who she was, and she had the audacity to answer my question with a question asking who I was. If you haven't yet figured out my personality, it's very strong. Needless to say, that was the wrong answer from this girl. I told her in a very firm voice, "Well I'm the daughter." She starts blabbering on about how my dad said it was ok, blah blah blah. I simply said, "Okay," and walked over to see my dad. She then left her washing post and called up Hank. She starts crying saying I was yelling at her and I was so mean to her. In retrospect I wish I had yelled at her because it would have been terribly entertaining. Regardless, Hank shows up, puffs up his skinny chest and tells me that he thought I was jealous that it was his girlfriend. (**Sidenote: This guy could not argue if his life depended on it). Then his little brother decides to call me to tell me what's up. I'm not entirely sure when and where these guys thought it was a good idea to call/confront me and give me a piece of their mind. It had absolutely no affect and I was still smiling. I don't know what they expected to get out of this whole scenario, but I rather had a fun time noticing that the stick up their arses must've broken.

Hank and I then proceeded to have a yelling match, yes I know, quite classy. One of the many foolish things he thought he would tell me was that the Sauer Family properties were not my property, nor the property of my brother and sister, AND other extended family. I think those family members would have a different response for Hank regarding that. That was one thing he really should have not said, among other things. Hank and I had arguments before. I was thinking that he surely would not have forgotten that I'm not fun to argue with, apparently I was wrong. So after his outburst about my family's property not being mine, and other mindless accusations, the really "mean, demeaning, belittling Jenny" came out and reamed him a new orifice by his rear end. Overall, Hank as a person isn't all that bad, but by him sticking around and not understanding what "breaking up" means really left a bad taste in my mouth. He's probably an okay guy as a friend, but probably not an okay guy to date.

# CHAPTER 10

# Ryan

In the fall, I took the semester off and moved to Chicago to model and attend the U of I affiliate there. I followed a guy up there, Ryan, and I also wanted to experience the city. He was a good excuse to go and I had family up there, so it wasn't so bad being there. Well this guy was a trip. I call this my "dumbass stage" in life. I did promotional modeling work and modeling for local boutiques. It was a fun time and great experience, but the modeling world is pretty mucked up. Since I'm naturally very athletically shaped, me being skinny isn't possible. So in order to make that possible, I didn't eat.

I had mono in high school so I knew what it took to not eat and you really get used to it after a few weeks. You just don't feel that hungry anymore since your stomach shrinks up. I would highly recommend not going this route because you feel like shit all time. You're always tired and moody because you haven't been eating anything. It's not a way to live, and I was pretty unhappy. I thought I looked great, but then my brother and parents noticed how thin I was and stepped in. They were disappointed and worried about me, so that was enough to wake me up and realize I was being stupid. During my first semester off, I couldn't take just modeling anymore and went back to school. I really liked school and doing only modeling was pretty boring and definitely not intellectually stimulating. I majored in biology and took as many literature courses I could. I probably should have majored in that area too.

I met Ryan while I was separated from Hank. A friend of Hank's tried to stir up some "shite" by saying I was cheating on Hank with Ryan. Yeah, that never happened. Hank and I were done and she was the ugliest red head I have ever seen, both physically and personality-wise. She also liked Ryan, think there is any correlation there?

Ryan was a big beefy guy and honestly was cute. This was the first jock-looking guy I went for and the last. Jocks have the stereotype of being "assholes"; if something is/has a stereotype, it's for a reason. His parents were divorced and his dad had physically and emotionally abused his mother. That should have been a major red flag. He also used the state system to get free college tuition by saying his dad wasn't around; just a real "shyster". Since I didn't really have any other solid friends at the time, I let this guy manipulate me. Me having such a strong personality didn't fit in this scenario. He also happened to be a total loser. He didn't have a car, stole money from his dad's change jar all the time, took money from my change holder, took a couple of my credit cards, and always drove my car. Why I stayed with this is beyond my comprehension. The only thing I can think of was that I was young and dumb. He had a younger brother, who didn't like me (it was mutual) and two other sisters. I liked his sister that was closer to my age; she had her head on straight. I bought him a computer thinking that he was going to pay me back, yeah, he didn't. One night, it was two in the morning, and Ryan called me telling me to go over to his place. I lived in my own one-bedroom apartment, pretty close to where he lived with a roommate that his whole family thought was gay. I'm sure the roommate was, but I didn't care, I got along with his roommate just fine. Anyway, I had made friends with the young drug dealer in my area where I stayed and slept. All I did was say, "hello" and ask how he was, and you know what? None of my stuff ever got stolen. It pays to be nice to people, and besides, he was just a kid. So I felt safe walking over to Ryan's apartment at two in the morning in the city of Chicago. I got there and he's on, technically my computer, and says that his roommate found a porn video and thought it was me. In that porn video, the girl is sucking on a stiletto heel and had many piercings in her ears. At first glance, yeah, she did look like me, but if you actually looked at it closely, you could tell it wasn't. One major thing, I thought, was that I've never mentioned wanting to suck on a stiletto heel, all I ever did was complain about having to wear heels. Also, another (I thought) very noticeable attribute, was that I have a double piercings on both right and left earlobes, not seven to ten like this girl had on her whole surface area of her ears. Ryan refused to believe me. I remember thinking to myself at the time, "What the hell is his roommate doing watching shoe fetish porn?" I got up to leave and Ryan wouldn't let me leave. He gave me his whole "schpeel" about loving me and other untruths, so I just stayed over there. Dumb, I know. My parents absolutely hated him, but at Christmas they still bought him gifts to make him feel welcome. I made my mom cry during this relationship because she saw what was going on and I just turned a blind eye. It was one of the most painful memories I have from that relationship, seeing my mother cry because I was such an idiot.

If your whole family hates a guy, they are more than likely right.

I wanted to come back home and finish my degree and decided to move back. I wasn't happy being with Ryan and I knew there was something up, but I felt like I didn't know how to get out. Thankfully I'm so close to my family that they convinced me to get out of there. The last straw was when I was over at Ryan's place one day and we were play fighting/wrestling. He did something to put my arm behind my back and I said that it hurt. Well he didn't stop. So I said, in a joking manner, "Okay Ryan, now we both know how strong you are, you don't have to prove anything." His response? He got mad. That is when I realized that this guy was crazy and he would beat the crap out of me if he could. I finally woke up and said I was leaving. He actually blocked the doorway and wouldn't let me leave. I told him I was going to call the cops if he didn't move. He moved after that, I left, and he wouldn't leave me alone afterward. He still had *MY* computer and I came by to get it, then he used this bullshit excuse of needing it and I would be taking away his only way of living and communicating for his "job." I just wanted to get out of there and didn't want to deal with it. My parents were ready to come up within a couple days to get me, and I had the locks changed on my apartment.

He came over one night pounding on the door and begged to come in. I let him do that for a while, and then the neighbors started coming out and asking what was going on, so I opened the door. We talked and he tried his crap magic again, and it didn't work. I told him I was leaving and that it was over. It didn't really go over so well, but I didn't care because I was finally leaving. Unfortunately, it didn't end there. I still had some "dumb" left in me. He ended up moving to where his mother lived, which was about an hour and half from me. This was an hour and a half from the small private college I attended as a senior to get away from crazy Ryan. His home was not in good condition, but he claimed he was fixing it up to sell for more money. This was something he always did; he talked a big game, but that's it, it was all talk.

He sucked me back in. I would go to visit him there, and he would visit me at my apartment near school. All of this happened behind my parents back. He was still the crazy old Ryan, nothing changed. He would tell me that I should move to Texas with him because my family didn't care about me. That was definitely something I never believed. He would also try and make me feel bad if I didn't want to have sex with him. Now I'll say this, I enjoy sex, with one partner, and whenever it is a happy, healthy relationship. The relationship with Ryan was not happy nor healthy, so he could suck his own "man piece" instead of trying to get a piece from me. He was a real winner.

# CHAPTER 11

# Frank

The next guy I ended up dating, Frank, was in my senior marine biology class at the small private college I attended last minute due to Ryan being a crazy mofo (slang for mother fucker). I saw Frank and thought he was hot. He and I started talking; although I was not in a relationship with Ryan, but I still talked to Ryan. For the marine biology's lab, we were to go to the Florida Keys for a week over spring break.

Frank was on a break with a girl and was using spring break to figure out if he wanted to continue anything with her. But over that break, I got close to Frank and it made it so much easier to completely rid myself of Ryan. Frank didn't really talk to me so I had to initiate everything, which was something I was very used to doing. We started talking in Florida and became very close, lying in the hammocks all bundled up and walking around together. It was a great time.

But here's a monkey that was thrown into a wrench (my way of saying "throwing a monkey wrench" into something. If you threw a monkey into anything that would definitely be a cluster of madness), Ryan threatened to come and see me when I got back from that break. I remember texting him saying, "If you do, you might get shot." Whether or not he would have, I don't know, but it was enough to scare him away. Ryan still needed closure and I said he could see me at my apartment. I didn't tell him that my mom and Ray Ray (my ex from high school) and Ray Ray's twin brother would be there. Ray Ray had just gotten back from a stint in Iraq, so he was ready for a fight. Ryan came by trying to make things better and talk his way back into my life, but it didn't work because I had such a great support group. He was also very intimidated seeing two big twin boys and my mom. Thank goodness they were there. After that, Ryan continued to call and text me and didn't get the hint that it was over. I ended up going to the police to file a report. I had all the phone records and everything ready to show that it was just him contacting me. The policewoman called him and told him to not contact me or further action in the case of a restraining order would be put in place. He quit, but he told the policewoman that I needed to stop contacting him. We had a little chuckle over that because we had the proof that he was indeed the crazy one. The lesson I learned here is that I now know what abused women feel like and why they feel like they can't leave. And here's reality, you can ALWAYS leave. I know most people don't have a support system like I had, but you know when something is wrong. There are so many options out there, such as women's abuse centers to call, but it's up to you to make the decision and find some smidge of confidence in yourself to get out. Guys like Ryan exist, but hopefully by reading this you can pick up more easily on the "crazy" in future guys that you meet.

So Ryan finally ended and Frank began. Frank and I grew close in Florida and became an "official" couple weeks after the trip. It was a wonderful time, but it was close to graduation in May and he was going on a 10-day trip to Europe with his family. He was also accepted to a graduate program in Little Rock, AR. We made things work and his twin sister, Sophie, was moving to Dallas and had no one to move with her. So she asked me. I said, "Yeah, why the hell not?" That's when my perpetual moving started.

Before I delve more into the relationship story, let me give you a little more insight about Frank. Frank was a year and a half younger than me, and the age difference became more apparent as time went on. There was always something wrong. Someone was against him and he was always the victim. Here's the thing, he wanted to make everyone like him. He had very low self-esteem, and it went back to his younger days in school. He wasn't treated very well by kids in grade school, but that happens to a lot of kids. The difference between Frank and a lot of kids that were picked on is that when they get older, they tended to get over it. Being bullied isn't a good thing whatsoever, I ALWAYS stuck up for anyone that was on the receiving end of being bullied. I know a lot of those kids that were picked on now that they are older, and they might still have a little chip on their shoulder, but the amount of aggression is significantly less now that they are older. Most of the kids I knew that were bullied went on to be more successful than the bullies, what a surprise. In Frank's case, I think it did more damage and he didn't feel the need to "fix" the problem. There was never any responsibility taken for his own actions, it was always someone else that caused something. He worked out all the time but yet felt smaller than everyone in the gym. He was built like a swimmer, he was in great shape and wasn't tiny, but it didn't matter how many times I told him, he still felt "small." He had a lot of potential, but he allowed all of those little kids to affect his psyche at such a young age. I told him time and time again that, "Only you are in charge of how you feel. Someone can affect how you might react and feel, but ultimately it is you who are in charge of your own feelings." I felt bad for a while, but when it's constant complaining and whining, the empathy starts to fade pretty quickly. I'm not without fault in any of these relationship stories, I know I probably did or said some stupid things, but I owned and took responsibility for all of them. I know when I'm wrong, I'm not about to pull the "wiener card' and blame it on someone else.

While Frank was in Little Rock, I missed seeing him and wanted to be closer. I also wanted to use my biology degree rather than just teaching fitness classes only. I obtained a research job in Little Rock and stayed in the same dorm building as Frank, but in separate rooms. It was a great way for us to get closer. We never had sex until I was in Dallas, which I thought was nice at the time. Frank was goofy and fun, we always joked around with one another and pretty much did whatever we wanted. Frank didn't have any really close friends at our old college, and I thought maybe it was the people there. All of his friends liked me, but I thought they just didn't understand Frank like I did. The same thing happened in Little Rock. Everyone he knew there liked me, but never thought of Frank as a "best friend" type. His only good friends were friends from high school. Most of the people in Little Rock were med students, which is what Frank had hoped to do.

When Frank told me he got into medical school in Oklahoma City, I was so excited for him because I knew that he wanted it so badly and finally got it. I was also excited because that meant that I got to move again! We were long-distance for quite a while until I found a job as a "fitness specialist" in Oklahoma City. Frank had the tendency to become really caught up with things and become really, inordinately stressed. He felt like he didn't have time to talk to me very much and devote much time to me, which he was right but to a point. I still tried to make it work because I thought I loved Frank when in all actuality, I was in love with the idea of being in love. Frank told me that we argued too much. Frank didn't like being wrong, and neither did I, but I really don't know anyone that truly enjoys being wrong either. When a topic would come up where I didn't believe something was right, I would say something. Frank would then become defensive because I didn't readily agree with him. Frank had been that way his whole life apparently. He was so embarrassing to be around whenever he would lose, or be in the process of not winning, during a board game, or with any type of game for that matter. Sophie and I would just sigh and say "whatever" and let it go. I never realized how stressful Frank was until we broke up.

Frank was telling me that he didn't know if it was a good idea for me to move to Oklahoma City. Well I didn't care because I wanted to be there with him. What I knew at the time, but would never admit to myself, was that I afraid of failing, failing at this relationship. When we were in the same place, we got along wonderfully. When we weren't in the same place, it was chaotic. He would call and complain about the people, the hard work, and just the overall stress he was having at the time. I would think to myself, "Hey, you knew what you were getting into, just try and make the best of it. You know how many other people would kill to be in your position?" He was too caught up in his life and his studies, and I couldn't take the constant complaining.

Again, I truly wanted to be there because I thought this was the man that I was going to spend the rest of my life with and have beautiful children with, *insert scoff, but I was terribly wrong. I met his OKC "friends" from med school. I liked most of them, and what do you know? They all liked me too. They would call or text me and Frank would always ask, "Why are they calling you and not me?" He was jealous! From there on, most of the calls or texts I received, I simply didn't tell Frank about because I didn't want to make him feel bad. I wasn't in a competition to make his friends like me more; that wasn't it at all. I started keeping those things from him because he was really upset whenever I received a notice, in the form of a text or email, from one of "his" friends because apparently they couldn't be my friends too. What he didn't realize is that I looked at these friendships as "our friends," not as "Well you met them first so they are your friends more than mine." I thought I was going to be married to this guy, so you have to get along with the friends right? Apparently they got along with me more than they did him. Boo friggin' hoo.

Here is one example, while living in Oklahoma City, of an experience with Frank that I have NEVER had with another man nor ever heard of from anyone else. Frank and I shared groceries, meaning that we split the bill half and half when grocery shopping. One day, we went shopping at a local Sam's, went back to his place and put all the stuff away. He then proceeded to add up the bill. I specifically remember this because I still can't believe this happened. I was sitting on the couch, across from him, and facing him as he was behind the kitchen counter. He then told me the total that I owed from the bill. I thought it was slightly high, then asked him to explain it, or I'm sure I gave him a, "What you talking about?" face. He said that he included the tax. I started laughing and asked him if he was serious. Oh, he most certainly was serious, he did in indeed add in the tax for what I owed him concerning my part of the groceries. Here's the thing: you do that with a roommate or friend with whom you may be cohabitating, not with a man or woman that you have been discussing living with and getting married to over the past couple years. I cannot believe a guy could be THAT cheap to actually add in tax to my portion of the bill. I've dated cheap, but this was just as bad as Ryan. Frank said in response to my laughing and questioning whether or not he was serious, "Well, it adds up over time." Well you know what Frank, when you said, "No" to me more than once after me coming into your study full-fledged naked to get some lovin', you can take that "extra, over time tax" and shove it where the sun doesn't shine.

After I was there for just about a year, I decided to finally do something for myself and move to Los Angeles. Acting was always a dream of mine, and I knew I was getting older, so I thought, "Why the hell not?" This quote and phrase is a very common theme in my life. I couldn't exactly start trying acting when I'm 35. Plus I moved to be closer to Frank three times. I thought it was my time.

At his behest, we ended up going to couples counseling before I left. The problems were the same things; he always thought he never did anything to cause them. I'm a tough cookie and I know I can be frustrating, but I thought I loved this guy that I never wanted to hurt him or make him feel bad, especially not intentionally. There always seemed to be this tiny level of competition between the two of us. I don't know if it was that way because we both didn't like losing, or because he actually was competitive with me. Regardless, we went and it helped a lot, I think mostly just helping myself to realize that it wasn't me and really was him

(**Sidenote; I highly recommend couples counseling. It doesn't mean that you have to be a really horrible couple to go, but if there is something that continues to reoccur during your relationship and you and your partner can't seem to work it out, go and see someone. The best thing is that they are unbiased and a great moderator. One day at counseling, I think we were doing some type of "rewording" where the other person said something in the terms that you understood it. For example, the counselor asked Frank to say something. He said, "I think you agree with Jenny all the time." The counselor asked him if he truly thought that and he said "no" and that he was just using that as an example. I still remember that so well because I knew he was lying. I knew he really did think that the counselor agreed with me most of the time. News flash Frank, I wasn't the one causing all the problems).

So I decided to move to Los Angeles. He visited me a couple weeks after I moved, and it was fun seeing him. Then, I started visiting him more often. Again, I always was the one to spend the money on flights to go and see him because he never had the time to see me. I understand medical school is busy and hard, however, if you have someone that you are talking about getting married to and love more than anything, wouldn't you WANT to find time to see them? Frank and I were together for slightly over three and a half years and he only came to see my family three times in Illinois. He also never offered to pay half or really anything for my flights to see him. My family had a tiny grudge against him because he never once came to a family function. I never felt he really cared about my family and really getting to know them. I tried really hard with his parents; I always sent them Corso's Cookies on special occasions, I spent a few holidays with them away from my family. I would spend a lot of time at their house. I later learned my dad said to my mom one day, without me knowing, "It bothers me that she's trying so hard with his family and he's never here." You know, that's a red flag out there ladies. Relationships are two-sided completely, give and take. Frank's mom wanted to always have the immediate family together all the time for holidays. I was never invited on any family vacations because it "might be the last time the older half-brother would be single." There was always an excuse, and I thought that was one of the dumbest excuses I've ever heard.

During the third year of our relationship, he and his family were going to plan a trip and what do you know? Frank's parents were extremely hesitant about me going with them. Frank finally stood up to his parents, and this was the first time during the whole relationship he actually stood up to them. They made a compromise that I could go with them, but only if I paid for my ticket and if they traveled in the United States. If they went internationally, then it was a "no-go" on me going. Look, I liked his parents; his mom said twice to me before that I was like one of her kids. So you would leave one of your kids at home while you took a trip with everyone else? That's how I felt. They knew Frank and I were very serious and talking about getting married. What would they have done once we got married? Every holiday Frank and I would have to be apart because they couldn't let Frank attend my family gatherings?

I'll give you a quick note about how my family treated my boyfriends. My family ALWAYS made the boyfriends feel like a part of the family. When I was engaged to Hank, my parents paid for his ticket and everything to Las Vegas when I went for my sister and my birthday (her birthday is the day after mine). They didn't even think of asking him to pay for anything because they figured "Well Jenny is with him and he may eventually be a part of the family, Jenny likes him and she may have more fun having him there with her." They did the same for my sister and her fiancé at the time; who is now her husband. Frank was always invited to anything we had, but he never made it because he just couldn't find the time. One would think at this point that he could've thought of a new excuse to use.

The other big sticking point with me about Frank was that he never stuck up for anything in his life, but he only did to me. He was this really happy, friendly guy to everyone else, but not to me. I saw all the times he was down and felt shitty, and I always saw the side of him when he puffed out his chest and stuck up to me. You know, it always pissed me off, and still does writing about it, because I thought, "Why in the hell can't you do that to everyone else that walks all over you? Why do you only do it to me and not to everyone else?!" He was a very easy target to pick on and take advantage of because he never says anything to make you think otherwise. There are going to be things in life that you don't agree with, so you can either choose to be a doormat or say something. He never grasped that concept. He would either not say anything at all, or just explode and become scarily angry because he would bottle it up for long periods of time. I mastered the art of saying what I feel without stepping on everyone's toes and thinking I'm crazy, but he never picked up on that.

While I was in Los Angeles, he complained some more about not having good friends. So I finally thought to myself, after hearing this almost every other day, "Ok, maybe it is actually HIM." I explained to him that he always tried to be the funny guy thus making no one take him seriously. He was never completely himself whenever we would go out and meet other people. He just had this "awkwardness" about him that people could pick up on, it wasn't really bad, but he wasn't exactly the same as he was around me. I'm the same with everyone, all the time. He maybe tried to be, but people can tell when someone is feeling slightly uncomfortable. He was a very good-looking guy and very nerdy, but that's what I liked about him. He was one of those that played "World of Warcraft", definitely not my style of game, however, we both played the game whenever we were apart because it was something that he loved playing and it was a way for us to "bond" and keep in touch rather than just talking on the phone all the time. It worked for us for a little while until I quit the game because I think it is truly a waste of money, and I didn't love it as much as he did.

Then came the momentous Halloween of 2010. I will give you the background of this evening because it plays into-spoiler alert- "The Breakup." Frank and I had a big fight a few months before Halloween. He thought about breaking up because he said that he didn't think he could be the best boyfriend for me and make me happy. Well he was right, but the jackass decides to tell me this the day before I leave to see him Oklahoma City. Good timing huh? The one thing about Frank, and I brought it up in couples counseling, was that he never said how he felt at the time. He would hold a grudge and keep it inside for two weeks to two months, and then bust it out whenever the hell he felt like it, thereby leaving me blindsided. How he could go on making me think everything was fine and dandy made me wonder about his mental stability. I tell you what, if I'm pissed about something, or I don't like it, I tell you right then and there. What's the point of keeping it inside and letting it brew? Maybe give it a day or two to simmer down, that's fine, but letting things build up inside you for so long? That's a bad idea in ANY relationship. Men and women, listen right now, if you are tired of this story and are just perusing, don't harbor ill feelings toward your partner for longer than a week. That tactic never turns out well.

This example is a good reason why to not give a silent treatment for over a week or two: I had no idea he was thinking that we should break up. I had just been there visiting him not too long ago; we Gmail video chatted a day before, and said that we loved each other on the phone the night before. Bascuse me? Where did this pile of cow dung come from? Was he bipolar? So I let him have it over the phone. I almost didn't go and see him, and looking back I wished I hadn't. My mom was also visiting me in Los Angeles at that same time, so she heard everything I said and thought this was a real douche move on his part, again, the night before I was to go and hop on a plane to see him in Oklahoma City.

Fast forward to Halloween night, oh this is fun. Frank and I were all dressed up. We went out with a group of friends, I'm sure he would've said "his friends" because he met them first, and we were having a great time…until…I got drunk. Two girls started to hit on Frank, and I overreacted. I can admit it, I know I did. Of course, I am so good at facial expressions that I didn't even have to say anything and the girls stopped. One girl said to Frank, "Is she ok?" Frank says, "Oh, don't worry about her, she's ok." To most people that response would've sufficed, but not to me. What this night did was bring up all of the times Frank never stuck up for me. I shouldn't have blown up, but I did. Shit happens right? I also drank a lot of truth serum, so that didn't help matters. I took this comment from Frank as him making me look like a crazy girlfriend and not sticking up for me. That is exactly what I told him. I also proceeded to tell him how he never sticks up for me and I'm sick of it, and that I wanted to leave and go back to his place. A friend of mine (I met on my own and not med school related) met up with me and she wanted to leave the bar and go somewhere else. I thought that would have been perfect because I wanted to leave as well. When I get mad, I want to leave and just be by myself. The last thing I want is to have the person I'm mad at touching me, and that was precisely what Frank did. Plus it was a total buzz kill. He was trying to hold me in place and make me stay at the bar. Ugh, I just wanted him to stop it! Just stop touching me! I know he was trying to be nice, I know he was, but he should have known from couples counseling that when I say I want to be left alone, I mean it. Give me a few minutes, or a day, but just let me be me. I just told Frank that I wanted to leave and go back to his apartment. I was tired of going back and forth; I simply wanted to get out of that place. I took off my shoes and strolled through "Bricktown" with my bare feet. Frank was nice enough to eventually give me his shoes to use the rest of the walk back; like I said, "eventually," he didn't offer up his shoes right away We get back to his place and he almost starts crying and saying that he is so sorry that he never sticks up for me. He really did feel bad and we talked about it. We discussed how it would be nice for him to try and do it more and that it's okay. I was there for another couple of days and nothing more was said about Halloween. Like normal people, I thought that everything was fine. I thought we got over that hump and discussed it. Oh hell no, I was terribly wrong.

(**Sidenote: I have never needed anyone to ever to stick up for me, but it's nice to know when you have a man (not a boy) by your side that you can count on no matter what to be there for you, even when you're wrong, and tell you that you were being stupid but that he took care of it. That is what I always wanted from him, I wanted Frank to grow a damn backbone and stop thinking that he can make everyone love him and make everyone happy. It's life, so good luck trying to make everyone happy).

The breakup: This story always makes me laugh. To this day, I have yet to shed a tear over this break up. Frank is now known as my "ex-girlfriend" and you will see why. I had already purchased my tickets to Oklahoma City, without the suggestion from Frank possibly helping with cost, while on Christmas break from Hollywood. I was going to see him on New Year's Eve and stay with him for a few days after New Year's Day. We had bought each other Christmas presents and our tickets for our New Year's Eve in Oklahoma City. We also had talked about being married and engaged at the very beginning of December. So reader, stop and think about this, would you think that there was anything wrong with Frank? That he was harboring ill feelings toward me? You make all of these plans and talk about being very serious, should you possibly think that Frank is pissed off at you? No, you wouldn't. I had even sent him pictures of engagement rings and he had a stash of money that he had been saving to buy me an engagement ring, he told me that. Readers, this was obviously a serious relationship. It was Friday Dec. 17, I remember it well because that was the original date I was flying home to Illinois, but I changed my flight. This was also the day he was driving from Oklahoma to Arkansas for his Christmas break. I had sent him an email the day before: "I'll call you on my way to Bloomington, IL but we need to talk. Please don't be defensive when we start talking, it's just discussing a few things, no need for anger."

What I wanted to discuss was my issue with him not trying very hard with my family. I truly did want to have a discussion and not a heated argument. I thought we were grown up enough for that, apparently I was the only one "grown-up." He told me where he was on the road and said he was about home. I had driven that route many times and he was far enough from home that he could have talked about it. Regardless, he said he didn't want to talk about it and if we could talk later. I told him that it really had pissed me off but that it was fine. Then came Saturday, like it always does, then Sunday. I talked to him maybe a few times for no longer than a minute a piece those days. By this point I was flat-out pissed because I wanted to talk about everything but he never gave me any time because his older half-brother was there at home with him. By the way, I don't think the older half-brother ever liked me, but it was mutual. We talked on Sunday night and Frank tells me that he wants to talk about some things too. I said, "What the hell do you have to talk about?" because at this point I thought everything was "hunky dory." He says that there are a couple things and Halloween. I just about had a bowel movement in my pants because I thought to myself, "You have got to be kidding me, that was about two months ago." We continued to text back and forth and he tells me that I drag him through so much crap and that he never deserved Halloween and that I resolved that night with myself but not with him. Well, it's kind of hard to resolve an issue when the other person doesn't even know it is an issue in the first place. Remember, we discussed it all that Halloween night and nothing else was said on his end that it still bothered him. I was tired of the texting and just called him.

He continues to tell me that we shouldn't be together because he didn't deserve to be treated the way he was treated on Halloween and that it was very "traumatic." Reader, this is my side of the story, however, this break up story is not one-sided whatsoever. All of this is true and factual of what this guy, who supposedly has a penis, said to me. I told him that I didn't know it was still an issue. He claimed that I should have known because he brought it up all the time. I told him he always brought it up whenever we were joking about things, so I thought it was a joking matter. He also told me that I pushed him that Halloween. Now listen, if I would have pushed him, I would have remembered it and I would have damn well made it a good push if I were to do it. I didn't, period, end of story. What he considered a push was probably me pushing him away because I didn't want him to touch me. Well get this, he told me that he "felt like an abused animal" that night. I was thinking to myself, laughing to myself actually, "You [Frank] really should have thrown your vagina away in the trash can." I'm very honest here, I about started laughing and he was being very serious. I couldn't believe my ears. The guy I was just talking about being married to actually said that I made him feel like an abused animal. Ladies, if a guy ever says this to you, please walk away. If you ever get in a fight, he is by your side, and really did forget to throw away his emotional sack, you better start brushing up on self-defense classes because "he ain't helpin' yo ass out." I just let Frank talk because I was being entertained. He then goes on to tell me that I made him "feel like a victim throughout our relationship." He also said that he, not "me Jenny," that he Frank wasted three and a half years trying so hard for us. Sorry, what, come again? Bascuse me, bowkay? Did I need to bust out my Beethoven hearing piece? I think you just stuttered because who moved for the guy three times? Who spent all their money moving and flying and making time for the guy? Yeah, it wasn't good ol' Frankie poo. So I asked in a very calm voice, "Ok, so that means I'm not coming there for New Year's Eve?" He says, "No." I then ask, "So does this mean that we are officially done on Facebook?" He says, "Uhhhh, wellll yeah, I guess." That still makes me laugh to this day that I had to ask that about Facebook, but he was all about Facebook and having a thousand friends that he didn't know, thereby making himself feel better about himself.

Ok, check. Then I ask, "What are we going to do about my things at your apartment?" He says, "I can reimburse you or send them to you." I said, "You definitely don't want to pay the amount, so just send the stuff to me. Ok, Merry Christmas" and hung up the phone. That was the last time we talked. I immediately went downstairs, told my parents, who looked like they could care less and my dad said, "You know, you always asked me if I liked him, and he was a nice guy, but he's an emotional lightweight." My dad's term is the best term to describe Frank: an emotional lightweight. Good job dad.

I severed the relationship status on Facebook, and that was that, or so I thought. The barrage of phone calls and texts were amazing. I had no idea so many people gave a hoot about my life. I got rid of Frank as a friend because I didn't want to see what was being written on his page. That's the easiest way to get over someone, get rid of the rubbish. Frank ended up blocking me, which therefore untagged him from all of our photos, which probably consisted of one thousand photos. I'm still working on clearing my "Frank and me" photos out on my personal Facebook page today. One of my really great friends, from Oklahoma City, told me that I make girls jealous. He said that every guy wants to date me and every girl hates me. This is something I could care less to know and could care less if that's actually how it is. He said that Frank probably blocked me to get rid of the photos because get this; Frank was in a new relationship not even three weeks later after we broke up. Nice twist eh? This helped me a lot because he made himself look bad without me even needing to assist. The new girlfriend of Frank's just so happened to be an ex. One of Frank's cardinal rules was that he never dated an ex. Well he broke that one. She also just so happened to be known to him and his family as "the crazy Jesus freak." He actually made fun of this girl to me. Sophie, at the time and this could've changed over the years, hated the girl and everyone else said how ugly the new girlfriend was and that Frank totally downgraded. Frank isn't exactly a player, so how he found time to cheat on me is amazing to me.

So Frank ended and Match.com dating began...

# CHAPTER 12

# Serial Dater

My mom called this time my "serial dating" stage, when I went on massive amounts of first dates from Match.com, so nicknames were a must to keep them all straight. Most of these dates happened while in Los Angeles. Los Angeles was a fantastic experience. Now would I ever live there again? I can say with 99% assurance no, however, I know of places I could live if the acting career took me back there. A pied-à-terre would be perfect in the city of angels, or Burbank-I love Burbank and Pasadena. Match.com was perfect because that's how I met people and made friends. I wasn't on there to find love or my next husband; I was too busy working on my new career path of acting. I decided to start on Match.com because Sophie had been on it and had a lot of fun. I didn't know that many people out in L.A., so I thought this would be a great way to meet people, do things, and go places I normally wouldn't. I logged on, paid for my subscription, and filled out my profile. I thought to myself, "This is fantastic! I get to pick out who I want and screen all the guys and say "yes or no." It's just like shopping! Who wouldn't want to do this?" I have included a few examples of men I met while in Los Angeles. The following chapters are some, definitely not all, of the dating stories that made life much more interesting and entertaining.

# CHAPTER 13

# JJ

JJ is one of the good stories. He was one of the first guys I met off of Match.com. I remember meeting him in one of the beach towns for sushi, and he was cute. He was a little more round than in his profile picture on the site, but he was definitely cute and I could tell he had a sincere quality about him. He was easy to talk to, and he told me later how nervous he was during dinner, but we had a good time. It was easy and fun. He told me about his childhood, and it definitely was not a good one, but the amazing thing about this guy, and probably why I genuinely liked him, was that he overcame a lot of obstacles and created his own business. I love hearing other people's life stories because it gives you yet another vantage point from the window looking outward and not judging people based upon looks alone. JJ is a great example of having such a good heart, but you wouldn't know it unless you stopped looking at the tattoos and saw that it's just skin, not who he is. The issue here is that I was trying a new career, needing to be selfish and get my own life together. We had a lot of fun, went out on the weekends, and went for rides on his motorcycle. My friends became his friends. JJ is one of those guys that looks intimidating, and yeah I have absolutely no doubt that he would kick someone's ass badly, but is really a big teddy bear. He is still a great friend today. I will always have love for him and care about him, but know deep down that it would probably never work because he's staying in California, and I'm not going to ask someone to give up all they have to move to be with me because it "might" work out, that's simply not fair, and I've been there before. My mom met him at one point and really liked him; she saw what I saw in him, that caring and sweet side that a lot of people might never see because they won't get past the tattoos. I get along with everyone, I don't care what ink may be permanently etched on one's skin, but being perceptive and seeing things in others that a lot of people might never see in another, is a gift that mom and I have, and I am forever grateful to have that gift. I will always hold out hope that JJ will find someone who truly appreciates him for who he is, not because of what he has. I still love the guy and know he deserves the best.

# CHAPTER 14

# Surfer Dog

I think he was 6'7" with blonde hair-this is and was the last guy I ever dated with blonde hair. I'm just not a fan of blonde men. I'm a brunette snob all the way. The height thing was the appeal; I love tall because I'm not exactly short. I stand at an athletic 5'8" without heels. He was basically as sharp as a marble. We met up in a beach town, went out for tapas, had a little bit to drink, or a lot, and then went back to his place. This is one thing I will say about myself, I am not a whore, not one bit, but this was my only one-night stand, yeah at age 27. I pride myself on thinking the act should be shared with someone you actually like and it means something, not just for a quick release, in more ways than one. Also, I can still count on two hands, and not have to use my toes, the amount of men I've been with sexually; I'm pretty damn proud of that. I think there are girls in junior high, nowadays, that have been with more men than I have.

Anyway, we watched a movie in his bed, he had a roommate (something I cannot stand in a grown man), and he started trying with me. I was fending him off pretty well for quite a while, but then he started kissing my back. Damn that was nice. I never had a guy do that and I melted like butter, I pronounce it as "buttah" in this situation. And I mean my WHOLE back, not just a shoulder piece, nape, piece of rib, but the whole damn thing. So I give him props because he got me good with that whole back kissing thing, but he wasn't a well-oiled machine upstairs [brain]. The best way to describe him was "oafish." I remember waking up early in the morning, and that feeling of "Ah hell, what did I just do?" It was before sunrise, and I had to take the 405 back, so there was no way I was dilly-dallying around because the 405 ALWAYS sucks with traffic. Most people in California don't get up before nine in the morning, so I thought I was fairly safe getting out of there early. He gave me a half-ass offer of walking me to my car, I felt so stupid and knowing I was about to do "the walk of shame," I just wanted to get out of there, and no, I did not want him walking me to my car. I'm pretty sure I left an earring there too, damnit. I got out of there and didn't look back.

A year or so ago, I actually had some phone calls from him. That was just odd, I definitely ignored them. This happens a lot, I don't know what I do, but apparently I'm memorable because I get texts and calls years after meeting someone, even if it is just once. Nice curse huh? I would prefer to not have that curse.

# CHAPTER 15

# The Spaniard

He was the first, and I thought, last Gemini I dated. The horoscope people claim that Gemini's are the most perfect match for an Aquarius. They need to research that again because they're full of it. I'm not a fan of dual personalities and not knowing what mood I will get that day, no thanks. Surprises in mood are not deemed good surprises by myself. This guy was exceptionally good looking. He was smart in the business realm of things, I won't say book smart, but smart enough that I was intrigued. He was older, maybe 36'ish? He tanned a lot, but hey, he looked good. He was very honest about who he was, so by no means was there ever this idea that it would work out into a relationship. It was fun to hang out every once in a while, I met and made a new friend from him, it was just easy. The one thing I couldn't stand about the guy was that he had a massive stick up his ass, and I mean a tree trunk that had a termite infestation. I think he was intrigued by me because I didn't tell him what he wanted to hear and wasn't stuck up his bum thinking the sun and moon revolved around him. He thought he was too good to go places, but I saw something very different in him. I saw his insecurities, his weaknesses and it's just a shame that he couldn't get past the Los Angeles lifestyle and be a good human being. I saw it in him, but there's only so much I can do, and am willing to do, to help get that out. He knew how to get women, and I'm sure got a lot, but I was one of the few, if any, that wanted to end the romantic part of our meetings. I just wanted to hang and not have to worry about it becoming more serious. If it were to become more serious, then it needed to happen soon, but I didn't foresee that happening in the near future; so I simply put an end to it. That's too much work figuring out where someone stands, either you know or you don't, and I'm sure as hell not going to wait around forever to hear about it. Spaniard and having a relationship, I'm not entirely sure why he was so scared of commitment; he had a good family and his parents were still married, but it's not worth my time or energy to make something work that isn't. It was amicable, there was no yelling, no shit talking or calling the other names, it was ADULT. I still think of him as a good guy, a friend, and I harbor no ill feelings toward him...I just hope he lets the "good guy" out at some point and moves back to New York to be with "his people" he connects with better.

# CHAPTER 16

# The Moroccan

This guy could have been a model for an Olympian statue. His body was breathtaking, incredible, stunning even, and he was the sweetest guy ever. I'm telling you, I've met enough guys that this NEVER happens: he was hot AND super sweet. Here was the problem, he was too sweet. It wasn't one of those "too good to be true" things, he really was a very nice guy. He had his own fitness company, and took me to an authentic Moroccan restaurant in Los Angeles. It was delicious; it was my first experience with that region's type of cuisine. He dressed well and was concerned mostly about me having a good time. As I write about him it STILL makes me feel bad because I shouldn't have passed on such a nice guy, but I had to because he was too nice for me. He wouldn't get that mad at a situation and told me we could work on me not getting angry and arguing with someone. This made me laugh because I'm not that quick to get mad, irritated yes, but mad takes a lot more work on the other person's part, but changing me from being a spitfire and quick-witted wasn't going to happen. My mom, sister, and I make fun of people the right way, behind their backs. We tell their life stories when they can't hear us, and it's all in good fun, it ALWAYS is. I need to be with someone like-minded, not nice to everyone all the time. I know that sounds horrible, but I have to have an edge of cutting, cunning, wit, you know, "Irish." He also told me that the men in his country, and in his family, treat their women like queens. He wasn't full of shite either; he really did mean this stuff. I ended that as nicely as I could, and I actually did tell him that I thought he was too nice for me. My mom was visiting at one point while I was seeing him, I think we went out on a couple dates, and my mom even felt bad for him because she knew he was so nice. But, and this is a huge BUT, she also knew he wasn't for me. I wish him the best, and I hope he finds a girl that doesn't take advantage of his big heart. Even today, as I write and think about this guy, I'd give him another whirl because his heart was so pure.

# CHAPTER 17

# The Writer

He was smarter, or at least had great grammar, which is something I am attracted to, so we chatted, and met up for coffee. He then offered on another day to cook dinner for me at his place. Sounds good to me, I'm not about to pass up a free meal. He was all into the "Crossfit" craze, which was attractive because that meant he was serious about health and fitness, but then again, he would get up around five in the morning, in order to do this…me getting up before seven in the morning is a feat in itself. I walk into his place and all of his shoes are lined up perfectly; I of course had to take off my shoes, which told me he was slightly OCD (Obsessive Compulsive Disorder). I have my OCD moments, but his shoe placement, along with other things in his place, told me that he has a problem with change and may not be good with being "easy going." He cooked a great meal, but had me eat while he was cooking. It was weird because I was sitting at the table eating while he was preparing the food; he wasn't sitting with me at the table. Eventually, he finished and sat down with me and ate like a horse, and that was slightly off-putting. Then we decide to sit down and watch a movie over on his couch. This was around Valentine's Day because he bought me flowers, which was very nice. As we settle down to watch the movie, we don't even touch each other, he sits on the other end of the couch, and I made a joke consisting of something like, "I don't have measles, mumps, or rubella, I was indeed vaccinated so I could attend school." He skooches (moves) over closer, and we ended up touching hands toward the end of the movie. Yes, I was indeed excited that we touched hands-that's how awkward it was. I think it was maybe 9:30 in the evening and he says, "Well I have to get up at 5am, but it was fun and we should do it again." I actually was getting kicked out at 9-9:30 at night, pretty sure it was a Friday night, if not, doesn't matter, and it was early. He walks me out to my car, and it was awkward because we hug and nothing else. So I just kissed him and say something to the effect of, "Well if you aren't going to do it," then I went in for the kill. What a kill it was because it was a romantic peck, if there is such a thing. After that, I was done. A simple little kiss is fine, doesn't mean it needs to lead to anything else. He's still a nice guy, and I'm pretty sure we're still friends on Facebook. I have nothing against him, but there's another girl out there that is right for him and his personality.

# CHAPTER 18

# Boomer

This nickname was short for "Boomerang," he was from Australia. This guy was such a piece...of dogshit. You will understand my very unclassy, crass way of describing him here in a second, and more than likely agree. He was from Australia, very tall again, had the cute accent, colored eyes, Suave commercial-like hair, and seemingly nice. We were dating for maybe a month. He had this whole story that he was divorced and had all this money back home and was working on getting it all back from his crappy ex-wife. I don't remember all the details because he was full of cat barf and the story was becoming more and more elaborate. Anyway, so I need to get to the good part, I decided to fly home for a week and gave him my keys to get my mail. Holy cow was I an idiot. Los Angeles is NOT my small hometown. I didn't have anything valuable in my place, on purpose. I lived in an okay place, but it wasn't all that great. So I knew by giving him my keys he had access to everything, but there wasn't much access he had because I took all of my important items home with me. I told him to pick me up at the airport when I got back. So while I was home, the phone calls didn't happen much nor the texting from him. I knew something was up, but I already knew I was going to break up with him (yet I still gave him my keys, ugh Jenny) so I let it go. I enjoyed my time at home and didn't give it another thought. So I'm headed back to the Burbank airport, he's ready to pick me up, and tells me he has a surprise for me. Okay, I'm not like most people; I really hate surprises, especially from someone I don't know all that well. I was a nervous wreck on the plane ride because I already knew I didn't want to be with him and now there's a damn surprise? I was a mess.

He picks me up, and I'm not relaxed. He starts to tell me that the surprise is that he cleaned up my place, washed my towels and bed sheets, and took out my trash. My ears went back like a damn hunting dog. Cleaned my place? Washed my sheets? Washed my towels? Now THAT is just odd. So here's the juicy part: come to find out, the next day, I was taking my trash out of my trash can, I can't remember exactly why, I must've thrown some smelly food in there and didn't want it to stink up my place, but when I pulled out the bag, there was a used condom on the bottom of the trash can. I can't make this shit up folks, the dumbass Australian forgot to get rid of the evidence, and he thought he did and was smooth about it. So all the while I was gone, he brought another woman into my apartment, and had sex with her in my bed. What a lowlife eh? Now, of course I was mad, but for some reason this time I wasn't enraged. My heart was thumping because of the audacity of this guy, and basically from the stupidity of him, and mostly the disappointment I felt in myself for trusting him.

But here's yet another lesson I learned from this, the only thing to do is to NOT do it again. Move on, move past it. Allowing him to make me so angry that I would lose my wits is on me, not him, I'm in control of that. However, getting him back is a different story. To add the icing on the cake, I found a contact in my hallway. He didn't wear contacts. I also went to my neighbors, took a shot in the dark, and asked them about the guy that was coming over to my place and getting my mail, if he brought a girl over with dark hair and that the dark-haired female was a friend of mine. That way my neighbors wouldn't feel like some major happenings just went down, or unsafe because of me bringing a guy around. Well, I was right; they said he did indeed bring a girl that just so happened to be dark-haired over to my place one night. I had a 50/50 chance of her being blonde or brunette because I knew he wasn't into redheads or geriatric women.

I called my crazy Bolivian friend, told her about it, and her reaction was totally "crazy Latin-burned-bitch" style, so I had to majorly tame down her response. I wasn't going to go into his place of work and cause a massive scene and slash his tires. That just makes you look bad and doesn't prove anything. Instead, I told him I needed to talk to him, he knew something was up because he was doing it all via text. He asked what was going on and wouldn't let it go; I then told him I found a used condom in my trash can and it obviously wasn't mine because I don't have man parts. He started making junk up, blah blah blah, and said he wasn't at work. Well the whole time we were texting this crap back and forth, I was driving to his place of work, which wasn't too far from my girlfriend's apartment. I pulled up on the side of the street, completely at the opposite end of the street where he worked, and called. Big surprise, he was indeed at work. I told him I was outside; I know he was feeling fucked, and not in a good way. I simply stood outside of my car, not making a scene, WAY far away from the store that had no customers in it, told him he could walk down to me and we could chat. He gave me the excuse of having customers, so I said, "Ok. Don't you ever call me, text me, or communicate with me in any way, shape, or form, understood?" He just said yes, I hung up, got in my car, and drove away. He had a basic understanding of my personality, but anyone that meets me knows to not make me mad. I've done quite well quelling the anger, and I've never been in a physical fight; apparently my "mom tone" and look in my eyes are enough to make them stop. My Bolivian girlfriend couldn't believe that I wasn't crying and I asked her, "What good would that do for me?" That would be a waste of tears, so I'd rather bash him among my friends in the privacy of my own home instead.

# CHAPTER 19

# Oily Taters

A man should never have better eyebrows than a woman. Yes, I dated that man, "Oily taters." He was older, and his skin was oily, so it looked kind of like an oily potato. It was probably from all of the tanning he did. He definitely got Botox, or maybe the generic version of Botox, I'm not sure, but his face kind of looked like an oily spud. He was a fun guy, really. He was really good about texting and calling. He wasn't a long-term match, but he was a nice guy to know and to have fun with, that being said, it doesn't mean you can't date these people, it just means to go in with an open mind and have a good time but don't think that "this guy" necessarily MUST be the one because you are tired of dating. I've never been one to jump right into dating and loving every minute of it, but it's something that one must experience.

# CHAPTER 20

# Dr. D Bag #2

Another date I had was with a doctor from Orange County, "Dr. D Bag #2." He was cute and nice. The date was great and we talked about seeing each other again. We went out on a Friday night and at the end of the night we were talking about our family health history. It was really funny to me because I started thinking to myself, "Next time we meet, are we going to discuss our bowel movements?" It might not be an important thing to think of when you just begin dating someone, but it is very important. No one wants to hook up with a genetic mess and have kids.

Then comes Saturday, like it always does, and we texted a few times. I sent him a text saying, "BTW, I hope u don't have high expectations of my dating skills. I pretty much suck because I'm not a fan of dating." It's true I'm not smooth, but what I am IS brutally honest. I never received a response. Sunday happened and I texted him saying, "I don't know if you're still interested, but my plans got canceled for today and wondered if u were free." His reply, "Hey! I'm actually back down in the OC (Orange County) and have got to run a bunch of errands today." I knew what that meant. If you were really taken aback by a woman, would you blow her off with the excuse of running errands? Like I have mentioned before, I don't play games. I texted back with, "Would u want to meet up again? Really, if you don't, it's not going to hurt my feelings." I also meant what I said. I would much rather know the truth, and it really would not have hurt my feelings. He said, "I would like to, but the distance might be an issue." Men, don't ever do this. When you're dating, it isn't just all about you. Please be considerate of the other person because what this guy did was totally a waste of my time. It's unfair to the other person, and this is why. He knew where I lived before we met up, and he should have thought about the distance before meeting me. I liked the guy, and we talked about meeting up. He then asked me about driving to Long Beach, and I said that was perfectly okay on my end. My last two texts said, "I appreciate your honesty, however, I believe if u like someone enough, driving 45min-1hour isn't a big deal. I thought we had a good time and thought u were nice." Didn't get a response, so in my mind I said, "Well this is why you are 33 and single."

# CHAPTER 21

# Nasty Old Man

This relationship wasn't a "relationship." It's more of an experience that I hope none of my readers will ever have the displeasure of experiencing.

One thing about me is that I seem to attract old men. I've been told many times before that I am somewhat of an "old soul," however; I don't want to get it on with an old man that is older than my dad. I'm sorry, mature aged men out there, but I'm 27 (at the time living in Los Angeles), I don't want 50. I would still like to have children and not have all the kids in high school think their dad is "grandpa." Here's my funny story about a really old man, and I mean he was old, 78 years old to be exact. I'm pretty sure he shit dust. He doesn't have a nickname because his real name really embraced his moth ball self. So this old man owns a very successful classic car business, and rents his cars out to celebrities. I met him one night at an event and just thought he was a nice old guy. I'm really into cars, so I wanted to go by and view the beauties, not his old dusty sack. I get there and start looking around and it's great. He then starts asking me questions about my sexual preferences and what type of lingerie I like and my size.

Then my ears went back like a cat and thought, "Ok what the hell is this old man doing?" We continued to talk and he continued to ask me questions that should not be asked. Some other questions were, "Do you shave down there and why?", "Do you like older men?", "Do you like girls sexually?", and the list goes on. He was just a perverted old man, but I really only wanted to see the other cars. I was honest in all the questions, but after some of those questions I knew I was never going to talk or see this old "perv" ever again. He asked to take me to lunch, so I said yes because I never give up a free meal. By the way, he asked me to drive over there because his Rolls Royce tire just blew out. He complained about how low my 2007 Monte Carlo set as he got in with his black orthotic shoes. Oh, and his hair was a sight to see. Just think of Donald Trump with a thinning comb-over; that was this guy. I ended lunch whenever he asked me, "So, does this conversation turn you on?" I about puked ALL of my food all over him and his final sale orthotics. I wished I would have really, it still makes me want to go and hurl in the toilet today. He continued to try and call and email me. Whenever anyone uses the word "snack," I cringe and this is why. One day I felt kind of bad that I ignored him and I should have continued ignoring him, but I answered his phone call. He said it was about six o'clock in the evening and wanted to know if I would like to go and get a bite to eat or a snack. Smooth moves grandpa. My mom said to me, after hearing this putrid story, "Jenny, it's okay that you are honest, but you don't have to be honest all of the time." Yeah, she's probably right as usual.

CHAPTER 22

# Magina

This guy was definitely special, and not special in a good way. Explanation of his nickname: he was a magician that had a vagina, not literally, but he was a sensitive bitch. He was seriously worse than a lot of my girlfriends. He was a narcissistic five-year-old, complained ALL the time, he didn't have good friends, and his family had a history of mental illness. Now you would think the magician part should already be a red flag, but the mental illness gene apparently didn't bother me. In all actuality it did, but I already knew this wasn't a long-lasting relationship so I never thought about it. He was also significantly shorter than me.

We met on a party bus going to a club for a friend's birthday party out in Los Angeles. Good thing I invited a couple other girlfriends because this bus was mostly just "hot girls"-that was the term used by the very few guys that showed up. I wasn't interested because for one thing he wasn't my type, and did I mention A MAGICIAN?! When I wear heels I'm either 6' or 6'1", and I'm going to wear heels out in public for an evening social event. Anyway, I also knew there was a solid chance I was moving

100

back to Chicago, so I wasn't looking for a relationship. Well, he zeroes in on me, lucky me, and I'm nice to him and continue to chat. He understood math and physics, so we got along well. While out at this club, The Spaniard and a best friend of mine show up together, so I go over and hang with them the rest of the time to get away from the magician.

A few days later, I start getting things together to begin the move practically across the country, and then magician starts texting me. I thought, "Oh why not? I only went on dates with guys that didn't have anything but cobwebs upstairs (there were a couple exceptions). I finally met a guy who liked physics, score! Yeah, then comes the part where the crazy starts to seep out like bad anal seepage you only read about in medical textbooks. In this case, it was rear-end seepage status. He came over to my place a few times, I went over to his place a few times, and we had fun.

I then moved to Chicago, and Magina and I continued to talk. He flew out to IL and visited the farm once, and then he got a gig on a show overseas. The site where he was to be was in a country I had yet to visit, so we both planned on me going over there while he was on the show. Now here's the thing with this guy: this was the first non-relationship I had. We weren't exclusive, and I was okay with that. I thought it was odd, just for a second, but if it didn't bother me, then that meant I really wasn't into him. If I cared much, there was no way in hell I would share my dude, but in this case, I didn't care. It was entertainment on a few different levels.

But then it all turned into a pain in my ass every time he would call, or Skype. He would complain about every damn thing and how he's so angry, has no friends, and how he still has yet to throw his sensitive man sack away in the dumpster to never be found again. This kind of sounds like Frank right? It's eerily similar, good thing I went through all the junk with Frank because it kept me "on alert." It also helped in the category of not putting up with any of it. One main difference was that Magina was smarter and admitted to having a mental problem. It didn't necessarily make the situation better that he was smarter than Frank.

(**Sidenote, I have always wanted to say this to guys who call someone a "pussy." Guys can't take a tap to the gonads, but a vagina? Now our lady parts can take a pounding. Can I get an "Amen!" from the congregation?)

He would call on the phone and we would Skype. This went on for about four months. I started to like him more, but I think those days were days I must've felt lonely because I didn't feel that way for more than a day. That feeling would pass by the next day, but I did e-mail him and tell him that I cared about him more, and I was looking forward to the trip. Subconsciously I was keeping him interested, in my own way I suppose because damnit, I was going to go over there! Well the trip was changed twice, so I had to pay the extra charges from the airline to change the date, and red flags had already been sprung. This wasn't a red flag, it was an, "Okay, now you're just starting to piss me off" red flag. I knew there was something fishy going on. I had already been on dates, and I did tell him that, while we were apart. That's what we agreed upon, and I could've cared less. He was kind of jealous about it, but that's because he cared more than he showed. You know someone cares about you if they ask you questions, just about daily life, and especially if they ask if you're seeing someone else. That tells the other person that they don't want to share you. Big surprise, I NEVER asked him because I really didn't have that deep of feelings for him (insert sad trombone noise). I'm also not saying all of this because of how things turned out, when you read on you will see that I wasn't upset at the outcome, but because this really is the truth, this is how it all worked. He was a good distraction, nothing more, and then he became a paper cut on my pointer finger. You know how those cuts are the worst? It's in a finger that you use ALL the time, plus it's a straight cut and easily opens up again when you make the slightest move! A band-aid placed on that finger is mainly a nuisance. You can't write properly with a big band-aid on your index finger, I don't care who you are.

One good thing that happened, I did get to meet, and got a picture with Larry King because of this guy...

Larry King and I at a party in Calabasas, CA.

Four months later, the final plan was to be overseas for the finale show with his friends, who were also going to visit from California. I arrived overseas, took a cab to the studio, and then we saw one another. Now remember, this was four months after not seeing each other in the flesh. We hugged quickly. It was the weirdest, most awkward damn hug I've ever had. I already had a gut feeling he was seeing someone else; I didn't care, but for shit's sake, try and be better at hiding it. Ignorance is bliss, that saying stands true here in this situation. I didn't want to know, so I was not going to ask a question that I didn't want the answer to.

Come to find out, my gut feeling was correct. But here's the dilemma: I didn't care but it's bad when I figured it out by seeing it, and I mean seeing it and noticing it right in front of my face. I will explain soon how my gut feeling was proven correct right in front of my face. If I decided to see someone, you know I'd have the decency to keep it all to myself right? It doesn't mean you're being dishonest, but if there is a mutual agreement where both of you can see other people, then seeing other people is considered okay. I told Magina when I went on dates, but not all the details. I never had sex with any of the dates, but I'm not going to talk about the conversation I had with my dates and how they had nice hair and eyes, whatever it may be; you keep that type of stuff to yourself, bowkay? If the other person asks for the details, then that's their dumb mistake for wanting to know. I would tell the other person, in this case Magina, if he asked for the details. I don't need alcohol, a.k.a. truth serum, to be honest; I bust it out if asked.

Rewind to a few months before this whole trip happened, he visited my hometown and met my physics professor. I love my old physics professor, and Magina claimed he had a major in Physics. Magina actually stole my professor's idea from my professor's work while my professor was on sabbatical. Magina had the nerve to use the intelligent idea as a trick in his portion of the show while giving no credit to my professor. You kidding me?! I'm glad I told the people who worked on the TV show how he "figured" it out. He was one of those guys that would take what you said, maybe you said something quietly or the other day, and repeat it to others as though it was his idea. He did that same thing once while we were in front of his friends. We were walking in front of his friends and I said something mildly humorous. He then slowed down and walked next to the line of friends and repeated what I JUST said maybe 30 seconds ago to them. He gave me no credit. Oh you know I wasn't about to let that go. I made sure to say loudly, "Yeah, that's what I just said about that building remember?" I can't stand people like that. He was also talked about very negatively in blogs, in the magician world blogs, about stealing other magician's ideas. I believed Magina when he said he would never do that, well, that belief got shot to hell after he stole my prof's idea without providing him any credit. Magina is one of those opportunists that steals from others for his own personal gain, be it very simply words, or genius ideas. He also claimed he was a genius. Well you know what? I'm actually at genius status, my IQ is 172. This is the first time revealing this publicly by the way, definitely not something I'm comfortable with but rather for the purpose of making a point. I obtained this number while taking a test during my freshman year in college. Granted, that number could have decreased a smidge over the years. However, I'm still smart enough to know when to shut up and not irritate people.

(**Sidenote: There is a fine line between low IQ crazy and genius crazy. The low IQ people really can't help their situation, but the genius IQ crazy get stuck in their head so much, therefore leading to narcissism and a multitude of other mental issues because they haven't learned how to control themselves and cope over the years, or have good role models-for example, having good parents to help teach them. My parents are very intelligent. My mom is naturally witty because she's Irish, but where dad got it from being fully German, I have no idea. I say that because Germans have been voted the most unfunny people for the past 50 years. My dad has some real zingers and is very entertaining. One can only be sarcastic and witty when all cylinders are firing upstairs. This will probably offend some people, but it's true. Lower IQ people and people with very low self-esteem do NOT understand sarcasm. That's why they say people that are sarcastic are mean people. Oh come on, don't even throw me that bone! If you can't make fun of yourself, you will hate sarcastic, witty individuals. There's always a slight truth to sarcasm, but if you can't handle the truth then you're going to have to work that out with yourself).

Anyway, the finale was over, he came out on top and won first place; then this girl came into the green room at the studio, and Magina introduced her to everyone in the group. Lo and behold, her name was Jenny. She was a dancer on the show and she had the trailer park/traveling gypsies nasty color of red hair, you know the kind you get in the box? And it wasn't the nice box color, it was the "on clearance because nobody would ever be dumb enough to put this color on their dome" color in a box. She was short too, of course, and then he took her into the adjoining room to "talk to her for a second." He actually said that. I have very good intuition and I can read people exceptionally well; this girl, Jenny, was one taco short of a combination meal, so reading her and her body language was a piece of cake. The celebrating was over at the studio, and after the show, we all left. I rode with Magina, and he then started to tell me that he was seeing this girl, Jenny, and explained it to me as though I was hurt. He had the whole "puppy dog, I'm sorry but not really" face. I told him, "You seriously couldn't have found another girl NOT named Jenny?" What's funny to me, and also at the time, was that was the only thing I found crappy about the situation.

So this is how I found out my gut was right: the day before the finale, I saw an empty condom wrapper in his trashcan. I told him this while we were in the car after the finale back to the hotel. He then got mad and asked why I went searching through his trash can. I almost flipped a lid, a trash bin lid that is, because here's one thing I'm not-a crazy bitch. I use face pads, Q-tips, hankies/Kleenex, and all of those used items go into the trash. Well, I think its common sense, but I actually look at the trashcan to make sure I throw it in the canister and don't miss it. It's also kind of hard to miss a metallic, shiny looking square condom wrapper on top of the trash, just sayin.' He decided to let that argument go because he knew me and he knew I wasn't the type to go searching through things, and also knew that I wasn't totally into him because we hadn't kissed at all, nothing. I'm pretty sure we only had the awkward hug as far as being intimate goes. A good ol' awkward hug, nothing says "romantic" like one of those.

He continued to tell me about his tryst with, "Bad Hair Jenny." He said it had been going on for about the last three to four weeks; what a surprise. That timeframe was precisely when I noticed he was acting differently via Skype and phone. I already paid to change the date twice with the airline, so I was damn sure going to enjoy this trip. He then told me that he had a sex addiction. Ok, what I say about those people is that they have commitment issues and are most often narcissistic people. Having or wanting sex all the time is not an addiction, I frankly believe that it's normal. I'm sorry people out there that claim to have this "addiction," but it's like some other disorders. There are a lot of diagnoses for every problem under the sun. I would be diagnosed with being Irish because I forget everything but the grudge. I don't need one thousand friends on Facebook to feel accepted, but narcissistic people do. Magina knew his friend count on his Facebook fan page every day. He would tell me if he lost or gained one person, as if this was something I really cared to hear. I would have cared to poke a dull pencil in my eye more, but I didn't. Magina said he had a sex addiction as an excuse to get out of an awkward situation.

We were supposed to go out afterward for the "after party," which was a combined celebration of the show being over and the host's birthday. It was supposed to be Magina, his friends from CA, and me going, but it ended up being just Magina and me going. Once we got there, I socialized all over the place.

I simply nodded my head and said "okay" about the whole situation. He talked so damn much he had skidmarks on his teeth. It sucked in person because I didn't have a mute button. I would use the mute button on my phone so I could finish other stuff while he was talking at me. It was great because he knew that I wasn't paying any attention to his story while on the phone. He also retold stories. I'm a pro at listening because my dad does the retelling of stories often; however, my dad is cool and actually tells a story as though he is talking to a class of kindergartners in the sense that he tries to make it entertaining, even after the fifth time hearing it.

We had arrived to this "after-party birthday party," and I started talking to everyone there. I had an amazing time. I even ended up meeting this comedian, William, who actually ended up coming over a year or so later to visit the States. There was nothing romantic, but he met my whole family, I'll get to him in the next section, but he was awesome and we still talk to this day.

Magina was sitting over in a corner with the other dancers; I think there were maybe three girls in the corner with him. That was it; he didn't talk to anyone else. I flitted about having a good time. I was there to have fun, not sit in a corner with three other girls and a magician. I have a feeling that last comment would be a great start to a joke. Anyway, I found a guy that said he had so much fun talking to me because he couldn't get over looking at and into my eyes, so he bought me many drinks and shots. I wasn't about to argue with him. I met the host, even though I knew he was a player from what Magina had told me, but hey, he bought me a drink, and he was an alright guy. William, this other random girl out on the dance floor, and I started dancing to the 80's music. I still remember there were so few of us dancing, but the three of us had so much fun we didn't care about anyone else.

So Magina, who will never admit this, got jealous that I was having fun without him. I didn't once go over to him, but then I saw him and "Bad Hair Jenny" go outside. I had enough because this was just flat out rude. Everyone there at the party knew I was there to visit Magina, even the guy that bought me a lot of drinks and shots because of my eyes. So I asked him why he and Jenny went outside alone together. He got all defensive and started bitching that she only wanted to have a cigarette. Well I have smoked cigarettes before, it doesn't take 20 to 30 minutes to finish one cigarette, even those massive long ones, I think the Virginia Slims or whatever? My reaction was based upon principle, as to how it is to treat someone. There weren't hurt feelings on my end but rather Magina just being an inconsiderate ass thinking he can treat someone this way, being rude that is, and thinking he could manipulate the situation to get out of it. I then decided to tell him I was going to leave. I got my coat, and started to leave. The magician, with a severe case of vaginitis, busted into the stairwell and started yelling at me that he wanted to talk to me. He said, "I'm not going to come after you again." I said, "I wasn't planning on you coming after me, when I tell you I'm going to leave, I mean it. I have a place to go, I'll figure it out, and I'm going to leave." So he turns on the "oh woe is me" chatter; I gave in because I really was having a good ol' time with William and company. We then went back upstairs; I was looking forward to forgetting about Magina and hanging with the "cool people." Well, Magina managed to mess up that plan, he told how he was embarrassed that I grabbed my coat and just left. Oh for shit's sake. HE was embarrassed? Ugh. He then took me into an adjoining room and started talking, then more talking, and still more talking. This is where I think of something that makes me sad, such as being in hell and my punishment would be to listen to this guy talk incessantly for eternity, to make me tear up because I'm tired, literally tired and exhausted because I don't care to argue with this narcissistic child. It worked, he shut up. Thank goodness for fake tears. We went back to the hotel, and chatted some more. His friends texted me to find out what was going on the next, well the little magician got mad that his friends texted me and not him; so I just went to bed. Tomorrow was a new day and I was going to spend it with his friends, thank the Lord.

So what happened with Magina you might ask? Oh…I will tell you with delight. Finally, the damn finale was final (like that set of wording?) and I could stop hearing him bitching about everyone and everything on the show. Oh yes, he was also always the "victim." At this point in my life, I was very much over "victims." All sense of feeling one bit sorry for this magic, yeast infection of a man was all gone.

Funnily enough, the day before, I had called my parents and told them I was actually thinking about coming home early because I couldn't take being around this guy. I decided, once he flipped his shit in the subway, that was it, I was going to head back to the hotel and spend the rest of my time by myself in a country I had never visited before; I will explain the subway episode here in a bit. I had talked to his friends about leaving early, and his right-hand man even said, "I think you're too smart for him." They all knew of his emotional issues and outbursts and were used to it. They completely understood what I was going through and while they weren't bad friends, they were still loyal to him in some way because they had known him for a long time. They were honest; I'll put it that way. They saw both sides, and it was wonderful meeting people like that because it wasn't awkward. They knew I was trying to have a good time and not make anything weird for anyone. That is one thing that I have been told by numerous people: that they feel like they've known me for years when they meet me. That is one of the most flattering things people have said to me; it's wonderful knowing that I can make people feel comfortable around me.

(**Sidenote: On one of the many plane rides I have taken, there was a black woman sitting next to me, she was hilarious. We both had a couple of fancy clear plastic cups of wine, and she said to me during the descent, "You have a good soul and a good spirit. I can feel and see it. You have this aura about you that is spellbinding and captivating; I seriously feel like I've known you for five years." That was one of the most amazing compliments I have ever received. It's not something I try and do; my mom is the same way. I see people gravitate toward my mom without her even saying anything, it's a crazy phenomenon, but I can see why the weirdest people in the room, the ones that no one talks to, come up to mom to ask her a question. She is a beautiful woman and intimidating to a lot of men, but somehow people will tell her their life stories within a matter of minutes. This is probably why my mom, sister, and I are so amazing at people watching and guessing their life stories. We've had the most random encounters of all types of people, so guessing people's life stories is an Olympic event for us, we live for that crap and are gold medal winners in that category).

Here comes the "subway episode": The next day I was out with Magina and his friends. I was already done with him, but playing nice to continue enjoying my visit. We were coming up from a Subway on an escalator, and he was staring at me. Well, since I'm already uncomfortable with ANYONE staring at me, in addition to counting down the days I wouldn't have to be around him, I said, "Why are you looking at me? He said, "Well I enjoy looking at you." So I said, "Well, whatever floats your boat." I didn't care, I couldn't care anymore. I wish I had a video camera because his response was priceless. I was laughing so hard on the inside because he blew up like the H-bomb; it was like watching a cartoon character get all red in the face and steam barreling out of their ears. He started complaining how I never can take a compliment, and I mean this heaping pile of dung went on and on! Being myself, I was trying to ignore the issue, i.e. let's talk about this later because we are out with your friends, but nooooo, it wasn't that easy. The little kid needed to continue his rant and wipe his bum on the floor like a dog to get attention. We were both staying in the same hotel room together, which by the way, no joke, we didn't have sex the whole time (thank the Lord). He made everyone uncomfortable and was mad because I was pretending everything was okay. His friends could tell what was going on, of course they could because he wouldn't shut up! I was still laughing and enjoying my time, let the little kid sulk in the corner, but if you rain on my parade for your own selfish reasons and can't pull yourself together for an hour or so, then you're on your own buddy. You can keep digging deeper into your poopy party hole because I'm not joining you.

All of us then went to another tavern, and I pulled him aside, outside, to tell him that I was going back to the hotel and he should just stay there and hang with his friends. I was horribly embarrassed, mostly because I was dumb enough to be seen with this guy, but also because he was making a complete joke of himself. He wasn't busting out any good magic there. I guess it would best be described as "disappointment in myself." He wanted to talk, shocker, so we did. All the while, this was happening outside of the tavern, so people were walking by; this wasn't in a secluded area. I started laughing at one point, and he got mad that I was laughing and actually asked me if I thought the situation was funny. Hell yes I said I was laughing and that I thought it was funny. He couldn't let it go that he wasn't winning the argument and changed; I mean a total 180, to being nice and attempting at being affectionate toward me. He said for us both to go back to the hotel and relax; he held my hand. It's a good thing it was winter and we were both wearing gloves. It was that feeling of wanting a shower after being touched by this guy, even just through gloves. Anything intimate with Magina was revolting to me, but I had to make it work so my visit wasn't ruined. I also had a piece of luggage that was shipped to another city three hours north of where we were, where he had to be the next day because he explained to me that he couldn't have THAT much to carry around on his pallet 'o' tricks.

We end up walking back, and he was trying to explain everything and kind of apologizing, but not really, then going back on things he said, then apologizing, then creating perfectly drawn circles (I'm imagining all those damn circles I drew with my dad's 1960s awesome compass in geometry class-this is an example of how my mind wondered while he talked at me). I just wanted to change my flight and go to bed. He talked about the damn problems with himself. Yes, with HIM. Again, why would there be any other life that was important other than his own and his own feelings? My life was unimportant at that time because he knew deep down that I didn't care a lick about him. I think the laughing in his face solidified that I didn't care about him too terribly much, or at least it should have.

Once I'm done with someone I'm done. That means ALL feelings are lost in addition to memories. Astrologists say this is a trait of Aquarians that they get over people quickly, be it friendship or romantic relationship. It is most certainly true. My viewpoint and I've shared this with countless others, is that why remember things that make you mad? Frank, the whiney doctor guy, I forgot his name after three months and we dated for three and a half years. This is because when I thought about him, it wasn't pleasant. Therefore, I forgot so many things about him and "us." People have said it's very cold-hearted, but to me, it's smart and logical. I still have feelings, and I let them out, but I'm not going to allow someone else to cause me to feel a certain way. That's all on me. No one, and I repeat no one, can make you feel a certain way, only you do.

I'll take a side step off my soap box now...Magina and I made it back to the hotel, we got into the elevator and then he tried to kiss me. Ooooooh man, I would have rather kissed a dog's worm-infested asshole than kiss him. I'm definitely not exaggerating. Even thinking back to it now makes me nauseous. Oh and I'm sure I made the "eating a lemon sourhead" look because I wasn't wanting any of that "magic." We finally get up to the room, which seemed like it took two hours just to get there, and he was being all nice and affectionate while I laid there with my arms and legs crossed on the bed thinking about: using a computer, where and how much the internet may cost, etc. I told him that I was leaving him early, and that we should both ride on the train tomorrow. I'll get my bag and then I'll jet. His ego was bruised, badly, and frankly I didn't give damn. I slightly enjoyed it because he was so arrogant, but it was also teaching him a lesson that he can't treat people the way he did me, and think that he can manipulate himself out of a situation. Listen up folks, you NEVER know who you will meet and should never judge them based upon their looks. I've met some of the most amazing people that look dumpy or can't match their socks, and most people wouldn't give them a second thought. Now there are stereotypes for a reason. Models for the most part are dumb, actors, well they aren't really known for being amazing scholars in math and science. It doesn't matter because there are ALWAYS exceptions to the rules. If you take the time and actually care about giving someone a chance, this is on a friend or romantic basis, it doesn't matter. You would be surprised at the amazing people and personalities that you will meet if you keep an open-mind. I have the most eclectic group of friends and I love them to death. JJ goes here, a guy that most people would be intimidated by, but is the biggest teddy bear and has a heart of gold. Okay, so he had a minor stint in "Juvie" (Juvenile Detention Jail), oopsie, but he is proof that people really can change for the better. I really don't believe 90% of the population obtains this trait to change for the better, but yet another example to be open-minded. Hey, you have nothing to lose by talking to someone, even the cashier in Wal-Mart. You are no better than anyone else; you are only better than those that think they're better than everyone else. They are just too stuck up their own rear-ends to see that it's not their world and everyone else is just living in it.

I should probably conclude this about Magina eh?

He agreed on the plan and did his annoying sulking thing. I went downstairs to the lobby; thankfully we were in a very nice hotel, to use the computers down there with the free internet. I changed my ticket, got a new hotel, decided to stay an extra couple of days. I had to get away from "Sulking Sad'gina'." I then went back upstairs to bed. This guy had weird sleeping issues too; I'm sure he heard me snoozing well enough that I wasn't worried about him. Dreamland, here I come!

The next day, we got up, checked out, and took the train to this other city. We sat next to one another, which was an awkward moment because I was thinking to myself, "Ummm, these are just train tickets, there are no seating assignments, go away!" I put in my headphones, pretending to listen to music so he wouldn't talk to me, and it worked like a charm. He moved across to the other seats and starting talking to some other poor innocent bystanders ears off about himself and his tricks. He was on a well-known T.V. show over there, and he loved the attention of people possibly recognizing him. It was always entertaining when people didn't know him and he thought they should.

I pretended to fall asleep. It was funny whenever the innocent bystanders started to sleep or turned around because they were exhausted listening to him. We had to make a train swap along the way, so we hopped on another train, and he sat next to me AGAIN! Son of a bitch, really dude? I said, as we were arriving close to our destination, "You know, this kinda sucks." He said, "What sucks?" I said, "Well this whole thing." Now granted I wasn't being completely honest here, but that was my attempt at trying to be nice. Why I would try and be nice to this guy was a mystery to me. He said, "Well you'll probably be over it in a couple days anyway." I said, "Yeah, you're right." It still brings a slight side smile to my face because he knew me well enough that I would be over it in a couple days; it was true.

I had the best trip, and to this day, it is STILL one of my most favorite trips because I made it fun. I didn't let this guy make me feel bad or ruin my time. I knew who he was and just rolled with the punches. This is what happens when you know and understand yourself, you can be happy without having others dictate when, where, and why you should be happy. I stayed for another couple days and traveled around by myself. His friends offered to have me hang with them, and I'm still thankful for their generosity, but I needed to be by myself and cleanse myself of all that mess that was "Magina." I'm still Facebook friends with his friends, and they were very nice people.

# CHAPTER 23

# William

William was a guy from overseas, whom I met while with Magina, and this wasn't a romantic relationship. This was a friendship and nothing was awkward. I'm including this because all of us meet others of the opposite sex and it doesn't have to be romantic! You really can be "just friends" with the opposite sex. William planned a visit to the states, and I organized a little trip for him. I wanted him to see a beach and such, but I was still new to working in Chicago for acting, so if I were to be called for an audition, I wanted to be in close proximity to Chicago in order to make it if need be. William scheduled being here for eight days. He got to see the farm, ride in my dad's awesome Chevelle, shoot a gun, watched dad make a microwave explode into smithereens due to placing a reactive target inside of the microwave, and then we went to northern Indiana to visit the beaches of Michigan, "Mich i gan" was how William pronounced it. It was fun; I won a vodka tasting contest at the little breakfast Inn where we stayed. We did nothing, we were friends and that's what made the trip enjoyable. We even slept in the same bed and he wore something like speedo underwear

119

around not thinking anything of it. Yeah, we literally just slept together. It was so nice being platonic and nothing weird, score! I took him to St. Louis to see the arch, the Budweiser brewery, and a Cardinals game. We stayed with my sister and her husband. Her twins had just turned one year old and he had a great time. My mom, sister, and I are still trying to plan on going overseas to visit him as well.

# CHAPTER 24

# Dingle

I came up with this name, even when I liked him, because there was part of his name that had "berry" in it; so naturally I thought of the word "dingleberry." That was how the family referred to him. He always wanted to know his nickname, but I assured him that he didn't. I suppose he will probably find out soon enough, shucks. He was a friend of a friend, lived in another state, and had just gotten a divorce. He was at a wedding, with his then wife, and that's when I met him. He was alright and was a good looking guy. He had some good, white chompers on him. He was getting up there in age, at least he made it seem like such a big deal getting older, but he wanted kids. He was jealous of my friend who had kids, had a good wife who didn't have five affairs on him, like dingle's now ex-wife (or at least what he knew of). Things started moving pretty quickly. He flew me out to see him a couple times and we had fun. His parents were amazing people. He was an only child, and I could definitely pick up on that whenever it came to him resolving issues with others. I think by not having siblings, becoming anxious, and knowing how to deal with that isn't as easy when being an only child, I could be wrong. I thought I was wrong one day, but then I was mistaken about being wrong.

He wanted to get married and have kids right away, and that was okay by me. I was at the point in my life where I was ready to do that, with the right person that is. Now am I going to seek it out and settle? No, but I would much rather date men that are at the same point in their lives as I am. He starts texting me, and yeah, HUGE annoyance with me was that he was 36 years old and ONLY texted. Ummmm, be a man and pick up the effing phone and call. We were long distance; wouldn't you want to hear the other person's voice? Maybe that's just me.

He would say stuff to me like he thinks "this is it," "our children," that kind of "thinking ahead, in the future" stuff. I went along with it because I knew he meant it. I trusted more of what he was saying and how he was saying it because I had references. I knew people that knew him, so I wasn't concerned about anything shady. He was great at texting, in the beginning. He would text right back, or get back to me in a timely manner, say good morning and good night, all that. Then, after about a couple months, he started to back off drastically. He owns his company and it's not THAT busy every day. I have friends that have told me about him not being overly busy at work. Dingle even told me one time that he perfected taking a nap so when the secretary walked in, she wouldn't notice. That tells me you're not always that busy.

I was on a trip with my mom, and I had to make him do FaceTime with me, which is ridiculous in itself. I shouldn't have to make my boyfriend want to see me. I think it was because he had pretty low self-esteem. I think it existed in him before, but after the whole ex-wife fiasco and how he claims she treated him, it most certainly didn't help matters. He was always worried about how he looked on the phone. That was so stupid to me because I did see him in the morning, so I'm not sure why he was so concerned. During this trip with my mom, I told him that I didn't think he is working at it anymore; this was when he started backing off drastically, which was only two months into the relationship. He said, "Well I thought we were at the point where we didn't have to work at it anymore." I couldn't believe he said that. He said later on down the road, that wasn't entirely what he meant. Yeah, bullshit. You should never stop working at a relationship. It's always work, but it doesn't have to be bad work. I want the guy I end up marrying to be pretty close to the same guy I first started dating. It shouldn't be like the show, "Who the Bleep Did I Marry?"

Time goes on and it's getting serious. He has the audacity to tell my friend that I was the one moving too fast. Bascuuuuuuuuuuuuuuuuuse me? I never understood why people deleted texts because I keep all that junk. It's like my dad and hoarding things because you never know when you might need them again, that's how I look at keeping a hold of all texts. He's the one that started in on the "let's get this relationship on crack" track, and I have the texts to prove it.

The texting continued to stay mediocre at best, and I was becoming so stressed out about it because if this guy was talking like he was to me and wanted to be with me, then why did he seem so distant? It was causing me a lot of stress because one day he would be very attentive and say the nicest things, then the next day it would be a total 180 in the form of radio silence. I seriously would not hear from him one day and sometimes two days in a row. This situation lasted for about three months.

I had a friend's wedding to attend, and he was going to fly in and be my date. However, the "up and down not really knowing what's going on" thing was driving me insane that I wanted to break up with him before he came. There was also the fact that he would never confirm and let me know if he actually was coming for the wedding or not. My parents liked him; he fooled everyone because all of my friends and family thought he was "the one."

Dingle and I hated the same things and had pretty much the same point of view on things as well. He was successful and good-looking. He was materialistic, and he used "things" to keep up the façade that everything was okay with him; when in all actuality he was an emotionally bagged-down mess. My parents convinced me to just see what happens when he gets in. I wasn't all that happy with him, but tried to talk it out and get it resolved when he arrived. I didn't understand why he was being distant toward me when I had done nothing wrong. Well, that harboring of ill feelings I had toward him played into the evening of the wedding.

We went to the wedding reception; he was already slightly uncomfortable that I was taller than him in my heels. We found our seating assignments and went around meeting everyone at the reception.. This was basically a college reunion for me and it just so happens that a lot of my friends at the reception were males. I was bound and determined to have a good time, so I did just that and forgot about Dingle. I really do feel badly about that, but I was still mad at him. I really should have gone to the wedding on my own.

The next morning was a mess. He was mad that I just left him alone and danced with my friends. He explained his side of the story, and I took full ownership of my actions and apologized. He knew I meant it, I wasn't blowing smoke up his bum, but he simply could not get over it.

Get this, I then find out, about eight months after I broke up with him (I still have that email), that it took him those eight months to get over the wedding night. Oh come on now! I wrote him an email admitting my faults and being very sorry for my behavior directly after the wedding, but it wasn't good enough for him. He even told me, at one point, that he does have baggage and that I would just have to deal with that. Oh no, I think not my friend. Your baggage is exactly that, yours.

I broke up with him the beginning of December, and it was a hard break up for me because I really did care for him. I honestly thought he was "the one," and I broke up with him because I knew it was the right thing to do. It wasn't necessarily that I wanted to, but I knew it had to be done. This was the only relationship that took me more than a few days to get over, it was about a month I would say, and then I was fine.

Those eight months later, my national commercial for "Swiffer Steamboost" aired. He texted me one day, and started puking up all of his emotions and admitting what he did wrong during our relationship. Funny how it took him eight months to get all of that purged, but I guess his therapist helped him somewhere along the line. It probably also helped that he saw me on national television. We went back and forth via text, and I was actually seeing someone (off and on) at the time, but it was just texting with Dingle, nothing more. And like usual, the texting stopped abruptly.

Not too long ago, about a month or so ago, he texted me again and was talking about us seeing one another. Well okay, I was down with that. I find out a couple weeks later, after the texting stopped from him again, that he was seeing someone and thinking about selling his house because the new girlfriend didn't want to stay in the same house that his ex-wife had lived in with him. At this point, I have been disappointed enough by him that that piece of news didn't even bother me. Also, I'm not about to be someone's backburner. So my family, like we always do, made fun of the situation he is now in with this new girl. What I have to say about Dingle is that he really is a nice guy, but he's very sensitive and needs someone on that same level.

# CHAPTER 25

# The Idea of Settling

Another point I would like to discuss is settling. I hate it, period. People that settle will always have some little piece of unhappiness in their lives. No one should ever settle, no matter how fluffy, unintelligent, or narrow-minded you may be, DON'T SETTLE. Let's say you aren't the prettiest woman in the world or the world's most sexy guy, you can still have standards. I have quite a few friends that have settled for someone over the years because they want to be married and have kids by a certain age. I know as women we have to plan for having kids at an earlier age because let's face it, our eggs get old. No one wants to take the chance on old eggs. If you happen to find the man or woman of your dreams at age 35, so be it. That's the way life works and be happy knowing that you didn't settle. You can sleep at night knowing you are with the man or woman that you always wanted to be with, and that should mean more than anything.

Another one of my life's mottos is to "live life with no regrets." I've been all over the place doing all different sorts of jobs, and I have loved every minute of it. I'm living my life and having a damn good time. One of the best feelings you can have is when you look back on your life and it makes you smile. When you have done that, then you know you are doing something right. I never do something half-assed, even if I fail; I know that I tried my best. I truly believe by me accomplishing all the dreams that I have set out to experience has made me a much better, well-rounded person. I wish everyone could think that way and have the same self-confidence to go out and accomplish their dreams. Don't settle down with a douchebag full of douchebaggery, be filled with happy little butterflies.

My current dating situation is this, a dry spell. I've been seeing a guy off and on, but it's nothing serious. I think it's one of those things where we both don't have a whole lot going on, dating-wise, so we chat whenever we have time. It works for right now; we shall see what the dating gods have in store for me in the future. I will also be turning the "Dirty 30" in a few days, and a fantastic quote from my friends Laura and Jim Hofman, "30 is one of the best decades in life ... everything seems to come together ... 30 is when you're young enough to enjoy and old enough to know better!" This quote is very true, and I can't wait to see what amazingly fun adventures I continue to have.

# CHAPTER 26

# Tips of What to Do and What Not to Do

I consulted with some of my family and friends to get a consensus of different viewpoints as to what is considered a good and bad idea for both men and women. *"It's all shits and giggles until someone giggles and shits."*-quote from a good friend about dating tactics and experiences.

**If a guy has better eyebrows than you**, forget it. He needs someone that is just as vain as him. When you notice this, it means a red flag has sprung and is flapping away in the wind. If you say to yourself, "Wow, his eyebrows look great, I wonder what else he waxes," then you might have a great time together. Look guys, it's great to take care of your eyebrows, but having them shaped like a woman's? Nah, not so much. I suggest getting them waxed, but just wax the uni-brow center and the fuzzy strays on the sides. You can pluck a few from the top and bottoms if they start to take over your whole eyelid and forehead. This same tip goes for those of you that have bushes for eyebrows, get them landscaped ASAP.

**Women, if you have a tattoo on your lower back**, you know what it means. It's called a "tramp stamp" by just about everyone. If you got it when you were 18, fine, however, if you get one when you are 30+, then that means you are indeed a tramp. I suggest getting a newer tattoo to cover up the original mess and attempting to make it look as pretty as it possibly can, or the best option is to get it removed.

**Now if you're a guy with a man stamp**, you probably play "World of Warcraft" and "Call of Duty" 24/7, on a regular basis, and have no need to continue reading this.

**If you have random hairs,** then fix it! Women notice those 15" hairs on the backs of your arms and shoulder blades, or the ones that grow erroneously out of your ear, nipples, cheeks, and so on. Pluck those for crying out loud. If you've been married for 10-20 years it isn't such a big deal, but if you're starting to get hot and heavy with a woman for the first time and this monster hair is staring at her in her face, I can guarantee you that she's going to remember that for a long time and it won't be a fond memory. If you want to make it to 20 to 25 years and still look sexy to your woman, take care of yourself. This also goes for women with the "Quasimoto" hairs.

**If you have bad gas,** try to contain it until at least after five to six dates. I think it's funny sometimes, but only if it doesn't have a horrid green cloud and causes asphyxia. Most women think it's gross, so be considerate. Once you let the big bomb drop, then you will be able to tell how much or little you can get away with in the flatulence department, based upon her reaction. If she starts gagging and yelling at you to go into the other room, then you might want to keep that methane wind tunnel under control. If she immediately starts laughing, you have a little bit more liberty to feel at ease to let the wind howl, however, be respectful and don't think that you can drop a doozey anytime and she will laugh. You do realize they can stink sometimes right? No matter what amazing music you can play with your ass flute, or how much you can make it wink, the smell is never funny. I really suggest taking Bean-o. I've taken it, I know it works. Look, women have gas and they poop just as much as you do. It would be amazing if a guy would make the woman feel more comfortable about letting out some of her awesome tunes. There is a product that you can spray into the toilet before leaving a load—it's oil-based and can really cut down on the "stank." If you know you smell like a rotting skunk that ate a lot of old broccoli before it died, be considerate and go into another room, don't let it go downwind to her, and please make sure it doesn't follow you whenever you climb into the car.

**Men, if you "jack off" a lot,** don't tell us about it, at least not if we don't ask you about it. Please lie when it comes to this. You and your friends may think its cool, but it's not. If you jack off in the shower every morning and before you go to bed at night, keep it to yourself. To us, that sounds like you have a problem. If you like it that much and can't get enough of it, go ahead and do it without letting us women know. It's not a turn-on unless you say, "I just 'got off' a few minutes ago so that when we have sex, I'll be able to pleasure you for hours." Now that's okay because it sounds like you mean it, even though maybe you just couldn't wait. Another thing, most women "get off" themselves and on occasion better than what you can do in the sack. If a woman "fakes it" during intercourse, just go along with it. DON'T EVER

ASK IF SHE FAKED IT! Seriously? Why would you even want to know if the answer is no? Once that happens, then you feel like a failure and your self-confidence just got shot to hell, and it's not coming back for a few days/weeks/months/years (you get the point). Oh yeah, and you just ruined a very pleasurable evening of the great "after sex sleep." I actually get tired after, much like most men. I say, "Don't ruin my nap. If you have something you want to discuss, we'll discuss it in the morning over my hot tea, but I'm nodding off because I'm pleasantly relaxed."

**Men, if you're emotional,** keep it under control. Being open and honest about your feelings is great, but don't expect a woman to be your mother and coddle you because you had a bad day at work due to overhearing your secretary say how much older you look than your actual age. "Shit happens." Maybe that's me being stuck in Freud's second psychosexual development of the "anal stage" or I really just don't give a shit…anyway, if you look older than your age, make the best of it. Work out to make yourself feel more alive instead of being a douche and buying an expensive sports car.

**If you haven't heard from her or him in a while,** give it up. Give it about three to four days. If they aren't in jail, in the nucleus of the Pentagon, or mayhaps taking a week in the Himalayas with the monks and meditating, then they're ignoring you. Take the hint. And please, for the love of God, do not keep sending text messages in the hopes that "Well they have to see those, so maybe they will respond." NO! Just stop, if they are not responding to any texts, then they are not into you. Plain and simple, black and white, stink on shit, etc. This can also be applicable to e-mail and Facebook.

**Men, if you play "World of Warcraft,"** keep it to yourself (see paragraph about "jacking off") until you get to know the woman, normally after you become "official." After you get to know the lucky lady, then shout it from the rooftops. Yes, there are some women that play the game, but more than likely, a high percentage of those women aren't reading this book and are meeting their future husbands in "Wintergrasp." I dated a guy that loved the game and played it every day. That was okay because he never mentioned it until after a while. It starts to get bad whenever the highlight of your day is when you tell your girlfriend that you tried out a new "Night Elf" character and dominated on PVP (player versus player) and "Hey, check out the new cool armor I got!" Not sexy, AT ALL. It's cute if it's talked about every once in a while, and I mean every once in a while stretched out for long periods of time. Overall, playing the game isn't a big deal, but don't bring it up until you have the girl so she gets to know you and she doesn't automatically put "madcap/strange/bizarre" on your forehead. If she leaves you after you tell her that nugget of information, then you two would have never worked in the first place.

**If you only talk through Facebook,** have your balls dropped? And women, where is your vagina? Really, if you have established that you both like each other, exchange numbers and pick up the phone. Who knows? The girl/guy you have been talking to via the web may have a voice of an 8-year-old cheerleader and you then realize, "I don't think I could take this voice for another 30 years." Another thing, send e-mails through Facebook. If you don't have anything witty or "cool" to say on his or her wall and their friends tell them, "Is that really the guy or girl you are interested in, because he/she sounds like a total dinkus". You don't want that, under any circumstances. Whether you like it or not, the family and friends HAVE to like you. The people that say, "You don't marry the family," obviously don't have a good relationship with the other fam. Same goes for the friends, try to kiss the arses of the friends and family. Trust me, it really works out in your favor.

**If your girlfriend has a "feminine issue,"** please be supportive. Look, periods, yeast infections and vaginal discharge happens, they just do. It doesn't mean that she is dirty and has problems; it's just a fact of life. The female pelvic region isn't pretty like an orchid, but hey, your penis and ball sack doesn't exactly remind us of Brad Pitt stripping down in a multitude of films either. Women know that men have issues of their own, but tell us just enough so we know that there is a problem and it will be fine. We ask the same of you. If we have something that really is gross, we will be considerate enough to let you know that visiting that happy place isn't going to happen for a few days. If you are a nice and understanding gentleman, then you will be supportive and not act like we have the plague.

**If you can't dance,** that's fine. However, if the person you are interested in likes to dance then let go of some of your inhibitions and try it out. Better yet, down a few shots to loosen up, that always helps. They will appreciate you much more because you at least gave it a shot. "The Carlton," is not a dance, but being silly and having fun is what is more important. If you bust out "The Sprinkler" and "Running Man" and really think its cool, then your date will ultimately be very embarrassed. They will also continue to only hang out with their friends and not ask you to come along when dancing is involved. If you are secure enough in that, then more power to you.

**If you like to clip your toenails while watching T.V.,** don't do it, at least at first. It's good that you take care of your tootsies, but it's kind of gross when you handle your feet, let toenail clippings fly all over, and then handle the remote with your dirty "feet hands." It's kind of like finding a hair in your mouth or food. Even though you know it's yours, it's still gross. You don't like finding random toenail clippings around. Keep it contained and do it in the bathroom over a trashcan, and please look around to make sure there aren't any stragglers. The same goes for trimming your fingernails, do it in the bathroom over a trashcan.

**Men, if you like to get a massage or mani-pedi,** no biggie. Men can enjoy those same simple pleasures that we women enjoy, and not be gay. Besides, gay men know how to take care of themselves, at least my gay friends do, and that is awesome. I enjoy a man that knows how to relax and is secure enough in his manhood to do these things. Now if it gets to the point where you have a weekly appointment, then that may be a little excessive. A man with nicely groomed nails looks good, however, if your nails look better than hers (if she goes au natural), then just like the "eyebrow tip," you need someone just as vain as you. In dealing with massages, get them. Even better? It's a lot of fun whenever the man wants to buy a massage for himself and his woman, or man's boyfriend or woman's girlfriend. It's a great relaxing experience for the both of you and thoughtful. You will probably then get some good sex for being so thoughtful and nice.

**If you have facial hair, keep it groomed.** Some women like the "rugged" lumberjack look, but only when it's under control.

Don't let it be very well known on the first date that you don't care because women look at you as if you can't keep your facial hair groomed and clean then you probably don't keep a lot of other things clean and organized. And women, if you have facial hair, I would highly suggest getting that problem taken care of immediately. I don't know too many guys that like a woman who has a faint 'stache' above their upper lip.

**If you have a lot of back hair and it starts to come out of your shirt,** get it waxed or trimmed. Guys, it's just flat-out disgusting. There are some women out there that love a hairy man, but most of us don't. If we see a tuft of hair popping out the back of your shirt, it just screams greasy and sweaty to us. You don't want that. The same goes for the hair that grows wherever it wants to underneath your hairline and the nape of your neck. Go and get a haircut/shave, please.

**If you have a lot of tattoos,** keep them concealed at first. Some men and women like it and some don't. Keep them under wraps and talk about having them on your first dinner date. This way you will be able to tell if they dig them or not. It's better to find out in person because you can tell by your date's initial facial expression.

**If your date has something stuck in their teeth or has a spot of something on their face,** then tell them. There is nothing more embarrassing than when you get into your car after a date and you see a big piece of basil stuck in your front two teeth. Your date might be embarrassed at first when you tell them, but I'm sure they would feel a lot better knowing that they, not the basil, were talking to you the whole time rather than that piece of basil talking at them.

**If you have big mole on your face or a massive zit,** try and see about fixing that before you meet. A mole on the end of your nose, in the corner of your eye, or by your mouth is distracting. I don't know about most people, but when I see that, I'm fixated on it. If you don't have the funds to get it removed just yet, which you should in the future, just please make sure there isn't a hair growing out of it. If you have a massive red protrusion filled with disgusting puss, pop it. There is nothing more revolting to me than this big red spot with a white head staring at me in my face. Come on, I know what's in there, get rid of it! This may sound weird to guys, but invest in a vial of concealer. If you have some problem red areas, just put a little dab of concealer on there and voila! Just make sure you match your skin color to the tube of concealer. It's easy enough; there are color maps in the aisles of makeup in department or discount stores. It doesn't mean you are wearing makeup, it just means that you have a problem area that will eventually go away, and you don't want that to be the main focus on your pretty little face.

**If you have drunk pictures that you think are funny,** do not post all of these with friends because then you just look like a party animal idiot. These are funny to you and your friends, not to potential mates that don't know you. One funny picture will show your personality and know that you want to have fun, not a drunken dolt photo. If you are still stuck in college mode, most will find that out later after talking to you.

**If you want to check out your date's Facebook profile,** wait until after the first date. It's nice to know what your date is all about, but sometimes when viewing Facebook the other person can get the wrong idea. They don't know you and if they view your photos, they could think that you are with many women or men all the time, or that you are a complete moron. For instance, a woman looks up a man's Facebook profile and sees pictures of him with the same woman in more than one photo. You don't know if that is his ex, which is what you will think at first, but in reality most times, it is his sister. You need to get to know the person first and then maybe you will have a better understanding of who they are.

**If you like performing oral sex on her,** ask her first about what she likes. It's very important in this area to ask your lady what she prefers and what makes her giddy with desire. If you go in for the kill and don't ask her feelings about it first, then you could be hailed as her knight riding in on a white horse, or be dubbed as that guy that slobbered all over her vag. If she's cool, she will give you another chance to redeem yourself, but not all women are the same in enjoying this. Another tip, don't be sloppy, that's just gross. My main thing is don't come up expecting to make out after you've been down on me...oh no, uh uh, I'm not about to make out with myself, that's disgusting. That's why it's important to ask first because some women care and some don't.

**If you like a certain part of you touched that makes you aroused,** then tell your partner! If you let them know what parts of your body you like to have touched or stroked, awesome. It makes your partner's job that much easier and will make you very happy at the same time. Women need to do the same thing for men. Women reading this, be honest with your guy and tell them what you like when you get to that point of the relationship. It makes it so much more pleasurable for both parties involved. Of course this isn't something you talk about over dinner, but bring it up at some point before. During the act, tell your partner then if that is a more comfortable time for you. It's amazing what open communication does in relationship. Plus, when you talk about it during the act, it can really heighten the experience for you both.

**If you're wondering whether or not to contact a woman or man on Match.com or any dating website,** read their ENTIRE profile first. For instance, if a woman is looking for a man 25-35 years old, don't email her if you are 49. If you honestly believe that you wouldn't have a chance in hell if you talked to her in person, then you more than likely won't have a chance in hell online either. It doesn't matter how much traveling, or how successful you are, it's completely out of her age range. If you are a few years older than 35, fine, give it a shot. Normally, if you are old enough to be her dad, don't send anything because that is disturbing. If the girl is a gold-digger, she will hike the age range up.

**If you aren't sure about calling or texting,** just do it if you want to. The whole "Oh I don't know, should I wait three days before contacting the person?" thing is stupid. Period, end of story. You need to think of this possible mate as a friend. You text or call your friends whenever you want to right? It should be the same for the person you are dating. I suggest not sending 15 text messages and calling five times in one day after just meeting. Relax and let it ride. Be yourself and do what you would like to do. If the recipient doesn't dig it, then they aren't right for you. There is no sense in acting like someone else in order to make the other person like you. They need to like you for who you are in order to have a long-lasting, fulfilling relationship. If you break out that you are incessantly crazy about calling and knowing where they are at all times of the day after you've gone on five dates, then they will just get freaked out and leave, or at least they should anyway. Five dates is about when you start to be more emotionally involved and you don't want to waste that time right? If you are a talker and love calling and texting, let that out in the beginning, slowly.

**If you just want to get laid,** then there are ways to go about it without being noticed.

- Women, I know we have that urge to just get laid without attachments, it's okay, guys do it too, but you have to be smart about it and think that is what you want ONLY. You cannot let emotions override. If there is a connection with the guy, okay. You can then decide to pursue that further at a later time, but not the night of. Do your thing and get what you want. You know how to get that, so don't cloud it with emotional urges or wants.

- Guys, do your thing. Do what you normally would to get the girl interested, but DON'T bring emotions into it in order to get what you want. Females can be very submissive to the emotional aspect, so don't be that guy who plays on the emotional card. This is a fine line, but you know what that is and don't pretend that you don't. Once the girl starts to show emotional submissiveness, don't play on it because then you have just crossed the line into "you're such an asshole" mode, rather than being the bigger person and walking away. Emotional scars are much, much worse than physical ones. Don't hurt someone out of selfishness, be smart and play fair. Be up front with the girl, and if she says she's down, then okay, it's fair game. If she gets hurt because she was lying, then that's her problem, not yours. The whole key here is to be honest, and if neither of you can be honest with the other, then either you are both right for one another or you both made each other have a bad night.

**If you're dating more than one person at a time,** it's okay, but don't be stupid. Keep your stories straight. If you can't, and/or you have had one "datee" question you, then check yourself. Don't be THAT honest, keep your game going but keep playing the open field. I've dated multiple guys at one time, but I played it smart. It's like playing chess, checkers, or poker. You don't give away your hand, and you need to keep the "game face" on. If you don't have one, then you can't have multiple dating partners at once. This goes for guys and girls. This means, PAY ATTENTION. Don't sit there looking into their eyes thinking you can read their soul. You can't. If you aren't learned enough in this category, then you don't know how to read eyes and the other person will be able to tell that there isn't anything going on behind yours. Be the master poker player and win this game! Check out their mannerisms, how they react to things you say, if they get sarcasm, what type of humor they may or may not have and see if they look down when you ask them a direct question, or if they look to the side. These are little things that might not seem like a big deal but they are when you are starting to get to know someone. The main thing here is that it should be fairly easy-going and keep your stories straight!

**If you have to work REALLY hard to make a relationship work,** then don't. Relationships are meant to be easy, not a constant uphill battle. Don't be "Sisyphus" and push that rock uphill just to have it roll back down. What a waste of time! Come on now, let the balls drop, man or woman, we all have them, just in different forms. I've been through this scenario, you work so hard because you want it to work, but obviously the other person doesn't care so much because then you wouldn't have to be working that hard, right? It's a natural occurrence, which is what a relationship should be. If you're putting in all the work, then drop it. Suck up that pride of yours and accept defeat. By the by, this feeling will go away after a while. I have a massive amount of pride, which gets in the way a lot of times, but as I have gotten older, I have realized that you need to bring that wall down, inch by inch, and you will see amazing things about yourself. Not only will you see a different reaction in other people with whom you interact, but you will see how much more relaxed this will make you. Pride is a dirty little thing, it can make you swell, and be so big and successful, yet it can bring you down like when your mom and dad tell you that they are disappointed in you. When my dad was upset with me for drinking at a young age, the sound and look of disappointment in his eyes were killing. I felt dead inside because I made my dad feel this way about me. And since then, I NEVER wanted to see that look on my dad's face directed toward me again. The same goes for relationships. Don't disappoint yourself by disillusioning yourself. You know when something is right and when it isn't, you simply need to keep your head straight. If you're using someone as a backburner, make it clear. That way, if the whole deal ends, then you aren't looking so atrocious. You don't necessarily have to tell them they are the backburner, but make it clear that you're not interested in something long-term and you're just having a good time. If they get pouty over it all, you weren't lying, you told them what's up. Tough noogies.

**If you have a fetish,** bust that out during the first act of intimacy...SLOWLY. You know how to gauge that stuff right? Don't bust out all of your fetishes because you feel like shouting it from the mountaintops, but rather, slowly introduce them. Ask the person little things and then you can see how far they are willing to go. Now I can tell you, I have no fetishes. I like a good ol' fashioned romp in the sack. No toys, no nothing, because in my view if you need those things, then you aren't doing something right. Besides, if a dildo gets you going, good for you, but I like the real deal and don't want to be disappointed when I'm with a man I love who can't do a "bob and weave" like your dildo does. Call me crazy, call me non-female, but I've never tried one and never will. I had a great friend from my college days give me one whenever I left the first university, and it stayed in the package. Maybe that's traditional, but hey, I want a guy that can work it, not a battery-operated deal doing it by myself. There are plenty of things to try and do without having to use anal beads. I apologize now if you're into that, this is all my personal preference, but metal balls in my anus, that is used for excrement, you know, nah, not really my cup 'o' tea. I'm not opposed to the idea of it ever happening, I simply am not a huge fan. Everyone has their own niche of fetish stuff they like, but approach the subject slowly and don't be overbearing. You never know, that southern Baptist may be a crazy toe sucker, but you can't ask that on the first date outright. Go slow, be patient. I will tell you, patience is a virtue, something I have yet to master, but when it comes to sexual prowess, practice etiquette and patience because you don't want to freak the person out, even if they may be a closet freak.

**Guys: "I hate women that constantly bitch about finding a good guy, then act like stuck up bitches unless you treat them like shit."**-quote from a good guy friend. Really ladies, come on. Don't make the rest of us look bad! I've heard this before from guys. Why in the world would you want to be treated poorly? It's not fun and it's definitely not okay. Nice guys shouldn't finish last, so change that foolish notion. I like the nice guys, I just happen to like nice guys that have a little rebellious streak in them and able and willing to stick up for me. I don't want a guy that ignores me; I'm too old for that nonsense and I'm not even THAT old. I don't want to play games, I don't want to muck around. I want someone that I want to be with and will indeed treat with me the utmost respect. I didn't even like this stuff in college. I've dated the proverbial jerk, who hasn't? It's up to you to learn from that and not continually go back to it. Why anyone puts themselves through dealing with someone else's jackass behavior is beyond me. Women, you're NOT another man's mother, he already has one. Even if under certain circumstances he doesn't have a mom, doesn't matter, not your problem. You're not his mother so stop acting like it.

**If you want to teach them a lesson,** fine, but don't try and change them. Men and women, you can both change, but it's minor. In a relationship, it's "give and take" AND work. That's why my parents are still married. How many times have I heard them both complain about the other? Well, quite a few times, however, I know they are perfect for one another and have worked their rear ends off to make it work. A relationship is a job, it really is. You have to focus and constantly work on it. I've said that it should come easy, but easy in the sense that you don't always have to think you need to change the person and make them like you. Keeping someone monogamous and crazy about you requires some effort on your part as well as theirs. I've watched my parents work over the years and they did a damn good job of it. Find someone that thinks of your best interests, not of their own because it'll never work out. Both of you need to be partners in all things. What is the point of life and not sharing it with someone? For example, traveling is always more fun with someone that you enjoy being around and love, not by yourself. Now I do love being by myself at times, but do I always want to be, in all aspects of life? Hell no. In times of greatness and in times of need, I want someone to share it all with me and not someone that I have to force to ask me about it all. You know deep down whether or not its right, but it's up to you to make that decision whether or not you're going to end it or put yourself through months, or years of misery.

**If you're a crazy clingy person,** don't be. You know if you're clingy and needy, you KNOW it! Don't kid yourself and think you're above that, that's poppycock. You know that you need someone and have to have someone all the time. Just own it for crying out loud. If you're needy, fine. In order to solve that problem, find someone that can put up with you being clingy and wants someone who wants them all the time. There is someone for everyone. If you need your space, like me for instance, then find a like-minded "needing space person." They ARE out there; it's a simple matter of trying and not just sitting on your couch watching reruns of "The Real Housewives of Beverly Hills." Not everyone is lucky and finds the best person that they are meant to be with for the rest of their lives on day one. It's all a thing of probability and statistics. The more people you meet, the better chances you have of finding that right person. If you're not into "going out" and looking to hit on someone, then go out with your friends. It doesn't mean you have to go out thinking, "Tonight, I'm going to find my husband or wife." If you think that way, you more than likely will go home terribly disappointed, or sometimes the power of thought can prevail and you find your lucky someone. I would say to not count on ESP, just be honest with yourself because once you are, then you will find someone that is compatible to you. Also, you find the person that is right for you when you aren't looking, 99% of the time. *I'm not siting any scientific data, it's called "Jenny Stats." A good way you can find out if the other person is clingy or lover of alone time, throw in questions or your "likes" to see what they enjoy. For instance, say, "I sometimes like to stay in on the weekend and watching a movie with a glass of wine." If you really do enjoy this, pay attention IMMEDIATELY to the person's reaction to what you just said, and what they say about it. If they hesitate, and say, "Yeah, you know, that's ok sometimes." Then ask, "Well, what would your ideal, or typical weekend look like?" There is no way to pussyfoot around this, it's a direct question. You need direct answers to figure someone out, not excuses and beating around the bush.

**Relationship talk,** this eventually comes up. The rule of not bringing up past dating history is an iffy one, with me anyway. I like to see how they approach the subject and how their body language changes, if at all. This says SO much about the person. I always ask the relationship history, the length of time, "What was your longest relationship and have you had relationships that last over a year?" If they are over 30 years old and have not had a relationship in over one year, I might be a little leery. You're not asking about what happened, they can tell you that if they want, or you can prompt it by saying, "Well was everything ok, simple break up" or "It's ok if you don't want to talk about it." What that says to them is that you're giving them the "okay" to go ahead but really you're being nosey as hell and want to hear the deets (details). I want to hear how they describe a person, if they are willing to be so open. This gives you more insight into the person, probably more than even they realize. You look at their eyes, which way they look and dart to, how their body shifts, what they're doing with their hands, where they place their feet, crossed at the ankle then cross at the knee, all of that stuff. AGAIN, PAY ATTENTION! Do not put your blinders on because they are "hot." Check them out all the while noticing what their reactions are to what you say.

**If you pick in your ear and in your nose,** don't. There really isn't much else to say about this, just don't do it in front of anyone. Do it in the privacy of your own home where no one is watching.

**If you're missing an appendage** be it hand, arm, leg, bring it up before the date. It's a touchy subject, no pun intended, okay, maybe that was a conveniently intended pun, but it's something you NEED to let the person know about while on the first date. Depending on the type of date you're on, it may not be as noticeable. For instance, I had a friend that went on a date to a movie theatre. The friend didn't notice that something was missing, and until both of them went to share the arm rest. Well part of the forearm down to the hand were missing, my friend was completely caught off-guard and really didn't know how to handle the situation (another unintended play on words there). She didn't want to be rude by asking about it, so it would have been nice to know up front in order to avoid embarrassing either person. It's not fair to keep them in the dark. Just be honest, they would more than likely be okay with it because you chose to be open about it beforehand.

**If you are a guy that loves short women,** never call the woman "cute." No woman really enjoys being called "cute" because that means that they aren't necessarily pretty but just kind of in a teddy bear cute, cuddly way. If you want to compliment the little lady, use words such as petite, beautiful, gorgeous, pretty, and along those lines. Whenever you and your vertically challenged woman get closer, then you can bust out the "cute" word.

**If you aren't the most romantic guy,** it's ok but try to be. I have been in relationships where the men forget to do nice little things, and any guy that does something thoughtful is always appreciated on my end. Here are some thoughtful and cheap things that you can do to impress your female:

- Send a random text in the day; it means that you took the time to think of them. That means a lot. Even if you only say, "I hope your day is going well!" that right there is enough to make her smile. It doesn't cost anything, if you have an unlimited cell plan.
- If you know her well enough that you have her address, pick up a card at Wal-Mart or Target and just

send a nice little "hi." It doesn't have to be all "lovey dovey" but again, it's the thought that counts and maybe cost you no more than $5. Now if you go to Papyrus and pick out a card, you are a winner in my book.

- I have said before, "Why would you send flowers when they are just going to die anyway?" Yeah, I got out of that stage and realized they are really friggin' pretty and really enjoyable to receive. If you send them to her place of work, buccu points to you! Even though she may be slightly embarrassed at first to have all of this attention, but believe me, she is thinking to herself, "My man really likes me and all of you other women didn't get any, just me." I do have one major piece of advice about flowers: Please don't get carnations. If they are filler, ok, but they are the cheapest flower out there and most women know they are. Yes, the thought should be enough, however, please be sure to add in some other flowers such as roses, lilies, and the like.

- Send an email with a quick little note. It's just like the whole text message deal, it shows that you at least thought about her once during your hectic work day, and oh yeah, BONUS!, it's free.

- If you are really busy and don't have time to talk for 30 minutes on the phone, still call and tell her you are busy but you would like to talk to her more whenever you have time. It shows that you respect her enough to let her know that you would like to talk to her, even if you simply don't feel like talking at the time.

**Men and women, if you text message a lot rather than speaking on the telly,** please keep the responses to your potential mate within a good, timely manner. In the beginning, you text right back, or at least most of the time. Try to keep the response within two hours. Nothing is more irritating to the "datee," and gets them thinking bad stuff about you, than when they receive a response four to five hours later. Really? You never checked your phone within that time period? I know you did. If you don't have anything clever to say, just make something up, that's better than nothing at all. This sounds ridiculous, but it looks like you aren't interested by waiting so long between texting. It's also a respectful thing to do.

**If you are a short man,** please be honest about your height. If you are 5'7" and go for a girl that is 5'7" she may not like that because women like to wear heels when they dress up. They like to wear flats sometimes, but when going out, most choose heels over flats. Besides, flats aren't near as hot as heels. Women feel more confident in heels because they make our legs look über fantastic, which is something you will be mesmerized by during the date, guaranteed. Most women don't enjoy being taller than their man when they go out because people stare, it never fails. You will always see someone point or look your way. It's a shitty situation and you can't help your height, but be realistic. Most women do not go shorter. They may go younger, but definitely not shorter.

**If you think putting your boyfriend or girlfriend down in front of their friends is a good idea,** WRONG. Maybe you're still a little mad over something and figure an attempt at being passive-aggressive is a good idea; you would be sadly mistaken. I have seen this many times where both men and women have a little chip on their shoulder from something that happened in a tiff, or the boyfriend didn't throw his socks in the designated bin. Whatever it may be, the angered person decides to throw in some snide comment to make themselves feel better. Not only is this a low-blow, passive-aggressive move, everyone notices, and I mean EVERYONE. The friends will take notice, and this will not help your chances of them liking you. The group doesn't care to hear about your argument. Plus, your boyfriend or girlfriend is placed between a rock and a hard place. They more than likely want to make a retort, but then also suffer the consequence of possibly causing a scene, thus embarrassing everyone in the group. If you have a bone to pick with your partner, do it in private.

**If your 'magic stick' does not fit in a magnum condom and looks like it's wearing a tent instead,** it's ok. Of course the bigger the better, but long and wide is the best. If you're hung like a horse, you probably don't have to read this book anyway because your reputation will precede you. It really is in "how you use it." You can't help the length, much like your height, but practice makes perfect. If you're good in the sack in regards to paying attention to her erogenous zones, you're good to go.

**If you find yourself starting to become comfortable in the relationship,** take a step back. I am a huge proponent of eating right and exercise. Just because you have someone, don't let yourself go. That's just pure laziness. Okay, so you put on a few pounds, no biggie. If you started the relationship out at 140lbs. and in a few months you are up to 170lbs., you better check yourself. This goes for men and women. Physical attraction is always going to be there whether you like it or not. Work with what you have. When you care about yourself, then you take care of everything else in your life. It really shows that you care enough to do something rather than sit on your ass for 15 hours watching episodes of "Battlestar Gallactica."

**Men and sweater vests:** How hard is it just to pick up the full sweater next to the pile of sweater vests, you know the ones that have sleeves? Come on, the sweater vest was never cool, and if you thought they were cool, you were probably a computer geek in 1984.

**Women, if you don't know how to put on makeup and want know how,** for crying out loud, cough up $30 and go to the MAC or Bobbi Brown counter and get some tips! That small amount of money, while yes it could buy you some solid groceries to last for about a week, if you're single, it will also give you knowledge that is priceless! These makeup artists can help you, that's what they are there for. Granted they will probably try and sell you a lot of products, but go in there having done some research. For example, look up what powder, lip smoother, bronzing facial blending brush are so you don't get hosed. This doesn't mean you need to do drag queen makeup every time you leave your house; some of those men are very good at makeup application bowkay?! Ask the makeup artist to give you a daytime and evening look, and you're set. Just DO YOUR RESEARCH and then you can make solid, sound decisions on what you would use most. It's comparable to men who buy tools. They didn't buy all of those tools at once in their massive machine shed, it took them years to acquire all those different things. That's how it is with women and makeup. You gradually buy stuff to add to your collection over the years, so don't think you need to buy everything at once, you'll get there. Plus most makeup brands offer free samples, quite possibly some that you might buy in the future.

**If you are not fully over your ex,** then don't start dating. Not only is it a dishonest thing to do, it is also completely unfair to your gal pal (vice versa for women). If she really starts to like you and can see being in a relationship, then you up and tell her that you aren't ready for one, then why in the hell did you start dating in the first place? If you're looking for a piece of ass, place an ad on Craigslist.

**If you're only looking for a piece of ass,** then you shouldn't be reading this book. Read above.

**If you enjoy talking about the nimrod you're dating with one of your favorite friends of the opposite sex,** don't. If your guy or gal friend isn't gay, they more than likely are into you for some reason. Hopefully they like you as a friend and keep it that way, or maybe they are waiting not to be placed in the "you're just a friend" category. Regardless, if you're dating someone that is a major pain in everyone's ass, especially yours, and you decide to complain to your friends about it, I can safely say they don't want to hear it. You have a straight friend of the opposite sex that cares about you, obviously because they are willing to sit down and listen to your complaints and try to help. Why help someone that isn't listening? If you're dating a major arse stain, then wipe that off! This friend of yours is looking out for your best interests and wants you to be happy, even if they aren't the man or woman for you. Don't go to them whining and complaining that you picked a dunderhead that doesn't care about you. If you have complaints about a man or woman being a real ignoramus toward you, you already know the answer: drop it.

**If you like sci-fi movies,** that's ok, sometimes. I myself like sci-fi and hate romantic movies. I really believe that it's important to talk about what sort of movies both of you like. It can show a little bit more insight about the other person. Now if a guy told me that he liked some romantic films, that's a "no-go" for me. Sci-fi is a dorky genre, but I'm a dork. Dorks seem to be attracted to each other like a proton is to an electron, we can't help it. However, I think that men should talk about their likeness for "Mega Python vs. Gatoroid" and "Bloodsuckers" after a few dates when things may get a little more serious. This goes back to the "WOW" paragraph, keep it under wraps until you can really open up. I did indeed just use the acronym for "World of Warcraft" right there.

**Women, if you enjoy wearing dark, heavy makeup all the time,** think about lightening that up ASAP. I asked a large portion of my guy friends, and this topic came up by quite a few times…and they all agreed. The main thing is that the heavy makeup should be held for evenings or special events. A "smokey eye" is not a daytime look. Most of my man friends said, "All a girl can do is screw it up with makeup. We don't know if she does a good or bad job concerning makeup application, but less is more." The "less is more" goes for a lot of things. Most men, and I say "most," but there are the vain exceptions out there, aren't that high-maintenance. Men may enjoy expensive toys, but for the most part, they enjoy a woman that can be herself and not have to put on a "mask of makeup" every day. Women, if you wear a hefty bag of self-confidence, you're on your way to being a walking piece of meat to all men.

**Women, if you fake cry,** make sure it's not all the time and ONLY used in times of desperation. In my case, if I fake cry, I have done it only because I was tired of arguing; I'm not afraid to admit it. EVERY woman has, just like EVERY woman has faked an orgasm. Again, let's insert the saying, "Ignorance is Bliss" here. What you don't know won't upset you. Now if it becomes a habit, well then one might need to reevaluate their situation. The more fake crying you do, the less effective it will be; don't get to the point of being ineffective.

**If you think you are finding a soul mate,** hold up a second. I really and truly believe that there is someone out there for everyone, however, I don't believe that you necessarily have a soul mate. I could fall in love with many different types of men and possibly live with a guy for 30 years and fall in love with another man somewhere else (that is if the 30 year guy passed away or something, not while still in a relationship). There are so many different types of people out there that I don't think you should believe in finding a "soul mate." What you should be finding is happiness.